The Promising God

Richard P. Bucher

DEDICATION

I dedicate this book to my family, whose love, support and encouragement enabled me to finish what I started.

CONTENTS

All citations from the works of Martin Luther are from Luther's Works. American Edition. 55 vols. Edited by Jaroslav Pelikan and Helmut T. Lehman. Philadelphia: Muehlenberg and Fortress, and St. Louis: Concordia, 1955-86.

ACKNOWLEDGMENTS

I want to give special thanks to my daughter Amanda Bucher, my son Samuel Bucher, my sister Kathy Boeckman, and my parents Rex and Nancy Bucher for reading over the manuscript and offering crucial suggestions for its improvement.

INTRODUCTION

This book is not what you think it is. It isn't just another book of Bible promises. The kind that organizes God's promises into categories with or without commentary.

Don't get me wrong. You'll find a flotilla of Biblical promises in the book. One whole chapter is devoted to explaining 50 of them. And there are dozens more.

But this book is more about the promiser than the promises. This is a book that focuses on the God who made all those Biblical promises.

Most Christians already know *that* God keeps his promises. *The Promising God* focuses on *how* God keeps his promises. It focuses on the typical way he chooses to get from point A (the promise he makes to us) to point B (making the promise come true).

Why should you care about that? Because if you don't know the method God uses in keeping his promises, you will see few of those promises fulfilled.

Knowing how God keeps his promises can be—and usually is—the difference between experiencing the fulfillment of God's promises or experiencing nothing at all.

Few things are more important for a Christian to know.

Yet—amazingly—a book about how God keeps his promises has never been written! Until now.

I wrote *The Promising God* for people like me. People who have often wondered to themselves why God so seldom seems to keep his promises.

On many occasions they have expected him to do so, but have come away disappointed and bewildered. Because by all outward appearances,

God didn't do what he promised.

For example, knowing that God has promised to give us what we ask in prayer, they have asked him for something they needed, and then waited. And waited. But nothing seemed to happen. What they needed wasn't given. And this kind of thing isn't an isolated experience.

Eventually they have reached some conclusion like, "What I'm asking must not be God's will for me." Or "God must know it isn't something I really need." Or "God must be displeased with me. He must know that I'm not putting him first in my life. Or he must know that I'm failing to do something he has commanded."

But conclusions like those are usually false conclusions. The real reason that what God promised hasn't happened probably *has nothing to do with you*. But it has everything to do with God.

It has to do with how he goes about fulfilling his promises. How he always has gone about fulfilling his promises. Strangely. Inexplicably. In a way that is frequently at odds with what anyone would expect.

In fact, God's method of fulfilling his promises and answering our prayers is so unexpectedly confusing that it leads most people to wrongly conclude that God has said, "No." So they just accept it and move on. And by doing so—tragically—they usually miss out on the fulfillment of the promise.

So what will *The Promising God* do for people like that? What will it do for you?

It will show you—with many examples from the Bible—how God fulfills his promises and why he does it the way he does. With this knowledge in hand you will know what to expect. And because you know what to expect, you won't prematurely conclude that God has said, "No."

You won't give up. You'll keep believing because you'll know that God is doing what God has always done. And because you keep believing, you will see far more of his promises fulfilled for you. And far more prayers answered.

Speaking of "Experiencing" . . .

Our culture is mad about results. We are a results-driven people.

God's promises definitely bring results. But they bring far more than that.

Consider this. All of God's promises involve divine intervention of some kind. In every case, God promises to *do* something for you. Rescue you. Provide for you. Give to you. Direct you. Strengthen you. Grow you. Show you. Heal you. Restore you. Empower you. Use you.

Calm you. Carry you. Be with you.

Every promise God makes results in his intervening in your situation or circumstances. Showing his loving presence and power. Revealing himself in your life. Encountering you.

So God's promises do far more than just bring results. They bring God. They bring God himself into your life. They bring his powerful intervention.

I believe that the deepest human longing is to experience God.

One of the most basic—but most overlooked—ways for us to experience God is to take him up on his promises. To take him up on one of his promises of prayer and then see him answer. To take him up on one of his promises of provision, and then experience his provision. To look to him to rescue us as he's promised, and then watch him do it.

One motivation to write the book was to help all of us experience the living God more than we have before. So if that is your desire, then this book will fulfill that desire.

No Matter Where You're At

Are you new to the whole idea of Biblical promises and wondering if this book is also for you? It definitely is for you! The first two chapters start with the basics. Explaining in detail—with example after example—that the God of the Bible always keeps his promises. Listing dozens of God's promises. Chapter Two alone contains 50 of God's promises—some of the greatest in the Bible.

Perhaps you know something about Bible promises but have never really used them. Never taken them for a test drive, so to speak. Is the book for you? Well, since Chapter Three teaches how to use God's promises, I can give an unequivocal answer. Yes! There is much here for you too.

Or if you, like me, have had a long-standing love affair with God's promises, and can't get enough, *The Promising God* is definitely for you, too.

Are you Facing a Problem?

What originally drove me to research the topic that became this book were the problems I was facing. Those problems motivated me to look up and use God's promises like never before.

So as I wrote the book, I was always thinking of people who may be facing a problem of some kind. Or who are in the middle of some seemingly hopeless situation. I wrote this book to give such people hope. To tell them, "God is still going to come through for you!"

Not Your Grandmother's "Book of Bible Promises"

There is something else I want to make clear. This is not your Grandmother's "book of Bible promises." It's not her daily promise calendar either.

A central theme in this book is that God wants us to be certain that whatever he has promised will happen. To expect it to happen.

Which brings us back to those little promise booklets and devotional calendars. You know the ones I mean. The kind that used to be found near the register of every Christian bookstore, and probably still are. I've got two problems with them.

First—and this is huge—many of them contain Bible verses that aren't promises at all.

I'm holding such a "Bible Promise Daily Calendar" in my hand right now. On the cover is the title, "365 Bible Promises." On the back it says, "*365 Bible Promises* includes promises and prayers that have been carefully selected from the Bible. Each new day offers inspiration from God's eternal Word, giving you a promise to remember and meditate on all day long." Sounds *promising*. But it fails to deliver.

In the month of January, for example, there are only two actual promises, and two prayers. The reading of January 2 is a typical selection: "No one can serve two masters. Either he will hate the one and love the other, or he will be devoted to one and despise the other. You cannot serve both God and money" (Matthew 6:24). That's a fine Bible verse. It's a saying of Jesus. But it is not a promise. Or anything close. Nothing is promised in it at all.

(In case you think that January was an anomaly, February only had six actual promises. March had only one).

The second problem I have with many Bible promise books is that some of the promises they include have been taken completely out of context, so as to entirely distort the meaning.

A recent example I saw included Isaiah 58:8 as a promise of healing: "Then shall your light break forth like the dawn, and your healing shall spring up speedily; your righteousness shall go before you; the glory of the LORD shall be your rear guard."

Now Isaiah 58:8 *is* a promise of healing. But when we look at the verses that come immediately before it, we see that the promise is not for just anyone. It is only for those who fast in a way that is God-pleasing. A fast that involves turning away from wickedness, feeding the hungry, bringing the homeless into one's home and clothing the naked (Isaiah 58:6-7).

4

So what appeared to be an unconditional promise of healing for anyone, turned out not to be when it was read within its context.

God Didn't Make His Promises Just to Make Us Feel Better

There is one last thing that has long troubled me. It doesn't have to do with the booklets and calendars themselves, but with the way that they are frequently used.

Over many years of speaking to promise booklet users, I long ago concluded that the typical user of Bible promise books is someone who wants to feel better. They are worried about something. Nervous. Lonely. Scared. Tired. Feeling hopeless. So when they read God's promises they make them feel better. The promises give them peace. Comfort them. Pick them up. Help them think positively.

Which is a good thing. Reading the things God has promised should make us feel better.

But what these users don't do, or don't usually do, is read a promise that God has made and then fully expect it to happen. Which is the whole point of God's promises.

If someone promised to give you $100,000, would you be satisfied that the promise gave you a good feeling? Not likely. You would expect the promised thing to happen. You would expect the person who promised to give you the money to *actually give you the money*. Otherwise the promise would be meaningless.

But in my experience many Christians are satisfied if God's promises make them feel better. But they don't really expect the promised thing to happen.

When the Christian Church says that we believe that God keeps his promises, we are really saying that we believe that whatever he has promised will happen. That is the primary point and purpose of all of God's promises.

In other words, we should treat God's promises the same way we do human promises. If someone we trust makes a promise to us, we expect that whatever he promised will happen. If it doesn't, it is a broken promise, regardless of how it made us feel.

How the Book is Organized

Part One (Chapters 1-3) is all about our Promising God and the role our faith plays in receiving his promises.

The focus of Chapter One is "The Promising God." In it I take a close look at the character of this God who has made all those promises. Because the trustworthiness of promises depends on the character of the one making them.

Chapter Two is "The Promises Chapter." I provide brief commentary on 50 of the Bible's greatest promises.

Chapter Three is all about the important role our faith plays in believing the promises. How most of God's promises only benefit us if we believe them. And the difference between faith and doubt.

Part Two (Chapters 4-7) focuses on how God goes about keeping his promises and why he does it the way he does.

Chapter Four examines God's promise-keeping method, part one.

Chapter Five reveals God's promise-keeping method, part two.

Chapter Six explores why God keeps his promises the strange way he does. Surprisingly, the Bible has a lot to say about this.

Chapter Seven discusses why knowing how God keeps his promises matters.

May this book make you certain that God always keeps his promises. So that you experience the fulfillment of more of his promises than ever before.

PART I: GOD PROMISES AND WE BELIEVE

CHAPTER ONE: THE PROMISING GOD

The very fact that you are reading this tells me that you like promises. That you view them in a positive light. So before anything else, I'd like to talk about what promises are and why they mean so much to us.

Let's start with this. Promises are different from most everything else we hear or read. And we hear and read a lot of words. So…many…words.

As a historian I can tell you that never before in history have so many words been spoken, written, published or circulated.

All day, every day, we're hit with a deluge of words – far more than we can possibly digest. Words transmitted to us through the spoken voice, through ink and paper or through wires and wireless signals. In conversation. On the printed page. Or on analog and digital screens.

But especially are we besieged and beleaguered by spontaneous words. Words that are unplanned, impromptu and off the cuff. Words spoken or written with little or no forethought. Words that popped into someone's mind that they just have to share right away. In tweets. Texts. Emails. Posts. Blogs. Or conversations face to face.

My sense is that there was a time when people thought more before they spoke or wrote. Those days are probably gone forever. Technology just makes it too easy to share any and every thought we have—immediately. Speak it. Type it. Click. Done.

Now contrast all those spontaneous words with the words contained in a promise. When someone promises something, in most cases they have given it quite a bit of thought. The words have been weighed and measured.

There's a reason for this. When someone makes a promise they are giving their word that they will do what they said. Which means that they are putting their reputation on the line. They know that if they break the promise, not only will they hurt or disappoint the promisee, but they will damage their own reputation. They might henceforth be known as a person who can't be trusted. Which is a serious thing.

Because of that, before someone promises something they will have carefully considered their words. They will have thought about the consequences, and the commitment involved.

So unlike most of the words we read and hear, promises convey gravitas. Promises are words that are serious and solemn.

There is another reason why we like promises. Why we are drawn to them.

Promises give us hope. They say, "The good thing I am telling you will indeed happen."

Whenever something good has been promised, we immediately feel better. Our spirits are lightened. Our souls uplifted. Our emotions calmed and brightened. We are encouraged, enlivened and emboldened.

Promises give us hope to keep going—and strength to overcome. They give us something to look forward to. Or cling to. They make us more positive and happy. Or they give us assurance that something bad that happened won't happen again.

So we like promises.

Mostly.

The problem, of course, is that promises are broken. All too often. For a whole variety of reasons.

Sometimes promises are made—and through no fault of the promiser—circumstances beyond their control make it impossible for them to keep them. Parents promise their children some marvelous vacation. Then mom or dad unexpectedly loses their job because the economy tanks. That kind of thing.

At other times the promiser hadn't fully anticipated all that would be involved in keeping the promise. And in the end he lacked the resources or commitment to keep it. Though you may disagree (and I don't blame you one bit if you do), many campaign promises fall into this category.

Or how about this one? Most of us have had someone make a sincere promise to us. That they will do something at such and such a time. Then they forget. It completely slips their mind. Or they oversleep. Or work gets crazy. And they don't keep the promise.

Another common reason for breaking promises is that the promisers simply change their minds. Because their mood changed. Or because something we did or said upset or disappointed them. So they change their minds and withdraw the promise.

Then, as we all know, many people make promises that they never intended to keep in the first place. These are malevolent promises. The promiser gives us their word about something in order to get something from us. False promises made in order to manipulate us.

Related to malevolent promises are the many "fine print" promises. A company promises some free bonus if the customer orders today. But then the fine print at the bottom of the page—or the speed legalize at the end of the commercial—state conditions so difficult to fulfill as to render the promise meaningless.

You get the idea. Promises are broken far too often for a whole host of reasons. Many more reasons than I can go into here.

But you haven't purchased a book about human promises, have you? You're reading a book about God's promises. And God's promises are different. Because God is different. God's promises are as different from human promises as day is from night.

There is a little known story in the Bible, recorded in the Old Testament book of Numbers, that profoundly illustrates this point. After the people of Israel had left Egypt and were on their way to the land God had promised them, they had to pass through the territory of several nations to get there. Though they asked permission to peacefully pass through, these nations sent their armies against them-- and were badly defeated by the Israelites.

So the people of the area—understandably–were afraid of Israel. The nation of Moab was one such nation.

But Balak, the king of Moab, had an idea. He had heard of a man who had the ability to curse people. A seer named Balaam. But unbeknownst to Balak, Balaam was a prophet of the LORD, the God of Israel.

Balak sent envoys with money in hand to invite Balaam to come to Moab and curse Israel. Balaam refused. Not to be deterred, Balak sent greater envoys with more money and asked a second time. This time, God gave his permission to Balaam, so Balaam went with them to Moab.

So Balak took him to a particular place and asked the prophet to curse Israel there. But instead of cursing them, Balaam prophesied an oracle of blessing. To Balak's considerable consternation, this happened four times. Instead of cursing them, Balaam blessed Israel, because each time God gave him a word of blessing.

But it is the second oracle that Balaam spoke that directly speaks to the whole question of God keeping his promises. Balaam prophesied:

"Rise, Balak, and hear; give ear to me, O son of Zippor: [19] God is not man, that he should lie, or a son of man, that he should change his mind. Has he said, and will he not do it? Or has he spoken, and will he not fulfill it? [20] Behold, I received a command to bless: he has blessed, and I cannot revoke it (Numbers 23:18-20).

In his oracle, Balaam contrasts the way God keeps his promises with the way human beings do.

"God is not a man," Balaam says, "that he should lie, or a son of man, that he should change his mind." God is not like people when it comes to the words he speaks. He doesn't promise something with no intention of fulfilling it. In other words, he doesn't lie or practice deception. When God speaks a word of blessing, such as a promise, he doesn't change his mind and revoke the promise. He never does this and nothing can induce him to do so.

Then comes two rhetorical questions with obvious answers: Has God ever said something and not done what he said? Or has he ever spoken a promise, and not fulfilled it? Obviously not! Because then he would not be God. He would be a man.

It is crucial that you understand this. It is a mark of his being God, a mark of his deity, that God always keeps his promises. Always keeping promises is an important part of what makes him God. An essential part of what makes him categorically different from humans.

Are you beginning to see? God doesn't promise something but then isn't able to keep it because of circumstances outside of his control. Because there are no circumstances outside of his control!

God never fails to keep a promise because he underestimated what it would take. He never underestimates.

God never forgets a promise. Never oversleeps. Never gets too busy.

He never breaks a promise because of moodiness. God is not fickle. He never promises something and then changes his mind because something we did or said angered or disappointed him.

And as said above, God never makes a malevolent promise so that he can sucker us into giving him our money or anything else. God doesn't need our money. There are no possessions that we have that he wants.

God never makes promises that have fine print at the bottom. Fine print so full of conditions we have to meet that he knows beforehand that he almost never will have to give what he has promised.

God doesn't make exaggerated promises and claims. He doesn't advertise deals that are too good to be true. What would be the point of that? How would that be to his advantage? He doesn't profit when people "buy" (believe) his promises. He gains nothing by tricking us because his promises are not intended to take something from us—as is the case with slick marketers. His promises are intended to give something to us.

What purpose would it serve for him to make grand promises, all the while knowing that because of the conditions that have to be met few would ever benefit from them?

No. Whatever God promises, he does. Always. Whatever God has promised, happens. Always. Without exception. In every case.

Many believers through the ages have found this to be true. They personally experienced it.

- Joshua—who led Israel after Moses--spoke to this truth in his final speech to the leaders of Israel after they had settled in the land of Canaan – the "Promised Land." "And now I am about to go the way of all the earth, and you know in your hearts and souls, all of you, that not one word has failed of all the good things that the LORD your God promised concerning you. All have come to pass for you; not one of them has failed" (Joshua 23:14).

- In his dedicatory speech in the temple, King Solomon said much the same thing: "And he stood and blessed all the assembly of Israel with a loud voice, saying, 'Blessed be the LORD who has given rest to his people Israel, according to all that he promised. Not one word has failed of all his good promises, which he spoke by Moses his servant.'"

One of the ways that the Biblical writers tell us that they have personally experienced that God always keeps his promises is by saying that his promises prove true. By "prove" they mean "tested" by experience, as metal is "proven" or "tested" in the fire of the smith.

- At the very end of his life, King David said, "This God-- his way is perfect; the promise of the LORD proves true; he is a shield for all who take refuge in him" (2 Samuel 22:31 NRS).

- In Proverbs 30, in words that echo David's, Agur, son of Jakeh prophesies, "Every word of God proves true; he is a shield to those who take refuge in him."
- The unknown psalmist who wrote the magnificent Psalm 119 said, "Your promises have been thoroughly tested, and your servant loves them" (Psalm 119:140 NIV).
- David writes in Psalm 12, "The promises of the LORD are promises that are pure, silver refined in a furnace on the ground, purified seven times."

Another way the Biblical writers attest to God always keeping his promises is by reminding us that God is faithful. In other words he is completely trustworthy. When he promises something, you can absolutely trust that he will do it.

- For example, the author of the New Testament book Hebrews urged the Jewish Christians not to give up by appealing to God's faithfulness: "Let us hold fast the confession of our hope without wavering, for he who promised is faithful" (Hebrews 10:23).
- Later in the same book he pointed them to Sarah, the wife of Abraham, and wrote, "By faith Sarah herself received power to conceive, even when she was past the age, since she considered him faithful who had promised" (Hebrews 11:11).

In all these ways the saints of old were telling us that the promises of God are completely reliable all the time. In so saying, they were enthusiastically recommending these promises to the rest of us, so that we can experience the same.

One Promise of God is Worth More . . .

I hope you are beginning to understand that God's promises are in a category all by themselves. Nothing compares to God's promises precisely because they are *God's* promises. They are *God's* words. Divine words carry more meaning, more significance and more worth.

One promise of God is worth more than all the promises of humanity from the beginning until the end of time.

No, that's far too weak. The *totality* of human words, all those written in books, stored on the Internet—distributed on a trillion Facebook and Twitter accounts, web sites and blogs—and all the clever, witty, beautiful, moving, novel, cool, hip, intelligent, new, brilliant, groundbreaking, loving words ever spoken, written, filmed or recorded, go up in the balance and are nothing when compared to one promise of God.

Every creative and brilliant thought of scientists, every groundbreaking legal decision of justices, and every pioneering invention of visionaries, recorded in billions of books, patents, research findings, dossiers, memos, laws, and journal articles are not worth as much as a single promise of God.

A single promise of God means more and is worth more than all the works of art produced and being produced by humanity, be they carvings, paintings, sculptures, architecture, compositions, poems, sonnets, songs, symphonies, photographs, videos or movies.

Art moves us, but a promise of God moves heaven and earth for us.

One promise of God also means more than all of your thoughts, experiences, circumstances, feelings, interpretations and sensory perceptions—as well as those of anyone who has ever lived or will live.

One promise of God means more and is worth more than any dire prediction you are making about your future, and whatever you think or feel is going to happen.

One promise of God means more and is worth more than whatever depressing thing that has happened or is happening in your life or in the world.

One promise of God means more and is worth more than whatever dispiriting thing that anyone has ever said to you or is saying to you.

One promise of God means more and is worth more than whatever negative thing you have ever said or are saying to yourself.

God's words are living, powerful and eternal. Human words are fleeting and ephemeral. Loud, chattering smoke that the wind snatches away.

When the winds of time have blown everything else away, the promises of God will still be standing.

If everything you ever trusted in has proven untrustworthy, the promises of God will still be reliable and will never fail you. When the storms of life have violently stripped from you everything you depended on, the promises of God will still be there, unmoved, unchanged, eternally dependable.

Get the idea?

God always keeps his promises. And his promises are in a category all by themselves.

As Certain as the Rising of the Sun

In Psalm 130, the psalmist finds himself in the depths of despair and in great need of help. So he cries out for God's mercy and help and forgiveness. Having prayed this he waits for God to answer. He tells us,

> "I wait for the LORD, and my soul waits, and in his word I hope. My soul waits for the LORD more than watchmen wait for the morning, more than watchmen for the morning (130:5-6)."

The psalmist doesn't leave us guessing what he's waiting for: "I wait for the LORD . . . and in his word I hope." Which means: "I'm waiting for God to do what he has promised in his word."

To illustrate his waiting more clearly, he compares himself to watchmen who, guarding a walled city at night, are waiting for the sun to rise. "My soul waits . . . more than watchmen wait for the morning."

That comparison begs the question, though. In what ways was the psalmist's waiting like that of watchmen? I see three points of similarity.

First, the psalmist and the watchmen had similar reasons for watchful waiting.

Why did watchmen wait for the morning? Because night was an inherently dangerous time. A time when invaders could more easily attack or infiltrate the city. The gates were closed and barred at dusk because night was a time of great vulnerability for the city. Danger and vulnerability not just outside the walls but inside too. Inside the city, the hours between sundown and sunrise were a time when someone could be up to no good, skulking about in the shadows to commit some crime.

So all night long the watchmen stared into the darkness, looking this way and that, trying to detect even the slightest unusual movement. The safety of the city depended on it. Nighttime was high stress-time for watchmen.

Understandably, then, dawn was a time of profound relief. It meant that the danger was over. It was practically thought of as a moment of deliverance. It meant that the stressful vigil was at an end.

That is why watchmen waited for the morning. For them, it couldn't come soon enough.

Neither could it come soon enough for the psalmist. As he cried to God "from out of the depths"(Psalm 130:1-2), it was the same kind of anguished waiting. Because he too was passing through a kind of darkness. A nighttime of the soul. He also was waiting for the sunrise of God's promise. When what God promised happened.

A second point of similarity is that what they were waiting for was definitely going to come.

When the watchmen waited for the morning, do you think that they ever doubted that the morning would indeed come? Do you think they ever fell into despair and gave up hope because they concluded that the night would never end?

To be sure, there were long nights that *seemed* like they were never going to end. But even then they were secure in the knowledge that nighttime always ends. The morning always comes. They would have told you that nothing is more certain than the rising and setting of the sun.

The waiting of the psalmist for God to come through for him was exactly like that. It was waiting for something that definitely was going to happen. Like the sun rising.

Oh it was still difficult for him to wait. As it would have been for the watchmen. Waiting in the darkness always is. But there was no doubt, no question, or no uncertainty that God would do what he had promised. There was no worry that he might not come to his rescue. It was as certain as the rising of the sun.

So if we think it preposterous to doubt that the sun will rise tomorrow, then we should think it even more preposterous to doubt that God will do what he says he will do.

If the thought of someone giving up hope that the morning will come is silly beyond words, then it should be just as silly for us to give up hope that God is going to do what he has promised. If we think it impossible and unimaginable that night will end and day come, then we should consider it just as impossible and unimaginable for God not to keep his promises.

The third similarity between the psalmist's waiting and that of the watchmen was the intense focus of their waiting.

The psalmist tells us that he is waiting for God *more than* the watchmen wait for the morning. He means more intensely.

What does that mean? It means that if watchmen peered into the darkness, counting every minute till morning would come, the psalmist did so even more. All his attention was fixed on the coming of God's help, and the keeping of his promise. He thought of little else.

If the watchmen did their watching faithfully, he did his more faithfully. If they were focused, he was more so. If they were certain the night would end and the morning come, he was more certain that his "nighttime" would end, and God's promised help come.

More Dependable Than the Universe

In the week before his crucifixion, Jesus talked at length about the end of this world and his second coming. One of the many things he said was, "Heaven and earth will pass away, but my words will not pass away" (Mark 13:31).

Now Jesus wasn't merely saying that his words will outlast the universe. He was saying that his words are more *dependable* than the universe. They are more reliable and certain than the existence of the universe.

Some think the universe is eternal. Jesus is saying it isn't. Some think the laws of physics are immutable. Christ is telling us they aren't. "But my words, all the things I have spoken, are," he is claiming.

Jesus is telling us, "If you think you can absolutely count on the universe always being there, you can't. But you can absolutely count on my words always being "there." You can absolutely count on everything I've said to come true and happen, including my promises.

But everything else will pass away. All the things in our lives that we think we can be sure of and count on, will all eventually pass away. Wealth. Health. Family. Friends. Lovers. Economies. Memories. Freedoms. All of them will pass away.

Fortunes are made and lost. Health gives way to sickness or injury. Family can be claimed by death. Lovers can betray. Economies can crash. Diseases can erase our memories. Nations and civilizations come to an end.

Only one thing will never pass away. Only one thing is absolutely dependable. That one thing is the words of Jesus. Which include his marvelous promises.

Character Does Matter

When it comes to God keeping his promises, character matters. In fact character is everything. But not our character. His.

This is so important to know. When we are waiting for God to keep one of his promises and it is taking far longer than we thought it would, the following thought process is typical: "Why is it taking so long? Have I done something wrong? Have I disappointed or angered God by something I've done or haven't done? Has he refused to grant me what I asked because I haven't been faithful?" Who among us hasn't had thoughts like these bouncing around in our heads?

But what are we doing when we think like that? We are assuming at that moment that God's keeping of his promise depends on our character.

What is character, by the way? It is the totality of a person's personality. All the personality traits that make a person that person. Including the person's ethics and morality. So when the culture tells us, as it often does, "Character matters," it means the kind of person you are matters.

Do you have integrity? Are you truthful? Faithful? Honest in all your dealings? Are you selfless or selfish? Sacrificial or self-indulgent? Decent or indecent? Lazy or hardworking? Thrifty or spendthrift? Generous or stingy? Careless or careful? Organized or disorganized? Loving or mean? Critical or kind? Judgmental or accepting? Reliable or unreliable? Clean or unclean? Responsible or irresponsible? Forgiving or unforgiving?

Now our character is important. And we should always strive to have a superior character. But our character is never what induces God to keep his promises, or what keeps him from doing so.

Which is very good news. Because if God kept his promises on the basis of our character, we would all be in trouble. The truth is, despite our very best efforts, our character is not always what it should be. It may be passable before people. But we know   the truth. More importantly, God knows the truth. He sees into the depths of our being. Every thought. Every motive. Every word. Every desire. He knows not only what we do, say, or think, but why we do, say or think it.

The standard that God holds our character to is far higher than the standard that people hold themselves to. His standard is succinctly captured by Jesus in the Sermon on the Mount, when he said, "Be perfect as your Father in heaven is perfect" (Matthew 5:48). God holds us to a standard of perfect character.

So it is indeed good news that the keeping of God's promises does not depend on our character, but his. Because the keeping of his promises depend on his character, we can always be absolutely certain that what has been promised will happen.

The First Thing We Must Know About God's Character

The first thing we must know about God's character—and the most important—is this: He sent his Son into the world to atone for our sins by dying in our place. That loving and gracious deed, more than anything else, defines God.

What kind of God is this God? He is a God who loved humankind to such an extent that he was willing to give over to death the very one who was more precious to him than any other. This was his *only* Son. His *beloved* Son. His Son from eternity. Who always had been with him.

Who do you love most? Imagine being willing to give over that person as a ransom to set a group of kidnapped people free. People who were strangers to you.

Imagine further that the people to be rescued were rather nasty. People that almost certainly would be unappreciative. Who might even mock you and your loved one, and what you did to save them.

Imagine that when you gave this person you loved more than any other as a ransom, you saw the captors torture him and kill him in the most methodically horrible way possible. You saw it all, from beginning to end. Imagine that you could have stopped it at any point, to spare him or her further pain. But you didn't. Because you knew if you did, the kidnapped people would not be freed.

Imagine all that and you are beginning to understand a little about God's love.

God's love is a love, in other words, that holds nothing back. Whose love knows no limits. God's giving His Son over to be crucified shows the lengths to which he was willing to go not to lose us.

If he was willing to do all that to redeem you eternally, do you think he is committed to you? Do you think he's committed to your welfare . . . your safety . . .your happiness . . . your needs . . . your life? If he gave his Son for you in such a way, do you think, maybe, that you are a priority to him? Do you think he would do all that and then care little or nothing about your life on this earth? Or is it more likely that he would continue to show the same committed love for you? A love that knows no bounds?

Are you getting it? How the giving of Jesus Christ to die on the cross is the first and most important thing to know about God's character? That if you are looking for something that most accurately defines God, that this is it? Good.

God's Character

What else can we say about God's character? Given that libraries could be filled with books written about God's character, I'll limit my comments to character qualities that are directly related to his promise keeping.

God is gracious. He is kind and good to us even though we don't deserve it. He doesn't love us because he sees something in us worthy of his love. He loves us just because he has decided to. He has saved us by his grace through Christ who died for us. He continues to deal with all baptized believers on the basis of grace. All his promises are promises of grace (Ephesians 2:8-9; Psalm 103:10; Romans 5:2,20; Romans 4:16).

God is faithful. Trustworthy. Reliable. He always does what he says he will do. He never changes his mind in a negative way. He never offers to give us something good, and then in a moment of moodiness or peevishness, changes his mind. God isn't moody. He is steady. Consistent. Always the same. He can be trusted. You can always count on him. Most importantly, that God is faithful means that he always keeps his promises. In the words of Hebrews 10:23, "Let us hold fast the confession of our hope without wavering, for he who promised is faithful."

One of the most comforting passages in the Bible is tucked away in Paul's second letter to Timothy. It says, "If we are faithless, he remains faithful, for he can't deny himself" (2 Tim 2:13). In other words, our failure to be faithful or to have the kind of character we should, doesn't change God's character. He remains who he is. Perfectly gracious. Perfectly truthful. Perfectly faithful.

God is faithful. And when he has promised something he *will* keep his promise. It is impossible for him not to.

God is truthful. He always tells the truth. He never lies. He never deceives. He never tells half-truths. He never withholds part of the truth. As we have seen, there is no "small print." There is no legalize. There are no secret or hidden conditions that are so difficult to meet that his promises become meaningless.

King David declared: "O Lord GOD, you are God, and your words are true" (2 Samuel 7:28). Jesus said of himself, "I am the way, the truth, and the life" (John 14:6). Paul calls God a "God who never lies" (Titus 1:2).

God is giving. This is huge. Permit me to expand on this character quality a little more.

God isn't tightfisted. He isn't stingy. He isn't a penny-pincher. He isn't someone whose default personality is ungenerous or grudging. He isn't someone who wants to keep everything he has for himself and for his own enjoyment alone. He isn't a hoarder. He isn't a Being who holds on to everything he has out of fear of becoming poor.

God is not a poor God. A God who has nothing to spare. Or a God who must carefully manage his resources so that they last, or will be enough to go around.

God is not like a wealthy misanthrope, who has the means to give, but because he hates all people, finds that giving nothing is strangely satisfying.

God is a generous God. He is munificent. Open-handed and open-hearted. He is magnanimous.

God loves to give. He lives to give. If it is true that God is love, then it is also true that God is giving. It is who he is at the deepest level of his personality. He is Giver.

God's passion is giving. His strength is giving. His gift and talent is giving.

He is the giver of gifts. Lavish gifts. Gifts that are bountiful and boundless. Gifts that fill up to the brim, then splash over the sides, overflowing. Jaw-dropping and magnificent gifts. Gifts that light up the eyes and fill up the heart.

His giving doesn't depend on people being *something* enough. Good enough. Moral enough. Holy enough. Loving enough. Generous enough. Hardworking enough. Smart enough. Religious enough.

Nothing makes God happier than giving. Nothing. Nothing brings him greater joy. The reason that there is "more joy in heaven over one sinner who repents" is because it is to such a one that God can give.

"God so loved the world **that he gave**" (John 3:16) is the best and truest picture of who he is. Unless we take it to mean that he gave in the past but doesn't give in the present. God so loved the world that he gives. God so loved the world that he will give.

God is not prodigal in his giving. He isn't excessive or wasteful. He doesn't indiscriminately give with no thought to results or consequences. He gives wisely.

His giving is timely. Always on time. His giving is ennobling. Improving the character of those who receive.

God's resources are limitless. The storehouse out of which he gives is infinite and immeasurable. The fountain of his gifts is inexhaustible, never in danger of running dry or running out. The ever-expanding universe could never contain all the treasures that are his to dispense. His giving is not limited by what he has on hand, or what he has in stock. Even if it were possible for God to not have, he is the Creator. He would simply speak into existence whatever was needed.

God wants to give. He desires to give. He longs to give. He yearns to give.

But he also wants us to ask. His giving is not limited to our requests. But he gives more to those who ask. He says, "You don't have because you don't ask" (James 4:3).

God is giving!

God is omnipotent. He is all-powerful. Nothing is too hard for him to do (Genesis 18:14; Jeremiah 32:17, 27). Everything is possible for him (Job 42:2; Mark 14:26) including the things that are, or seem, impossible to us (Zechariah 8:6 NRS; Luke 18:27). Nothing is impossible for him—except for one thing. It is impossible for him to fail to keep his promises!

Therefore . . .

Therefore, we should never worry that God has withdrawn his promise because we haven't been faithful enough, or good enough, or loving enough, or selfless enough, or generous enough, or moral enough. Because the keeping of all his promises does not depend on our character. The fulfillment of his promises always and only depends on his character.

Now in no way do I want this to be understood to be saying that it doesn't matter how we live our lives. That we can sin as much as we want, ignore and reject God's will whenever convenient, and God will still bless us, etc.

God doesn't "wink" at sin. It grieves him. It angers him. So, as the Bible teaches, when we recognize that we have fallen short of what God expects, and that there has been a breach in our character, we should repent. We should confess our sins to God and ask him to forgive us. Then we should believe the Gospel, that because Christ died for all our sins, the sins we have committed were forgiven at the cross. And we should always be striving to have the kind of character God looks for.

But the keeping of God's promises never, ever depends on our character. It always and only depends on his.

The fulfillment of God's promises depends on what Jesus Christ has done for us, not on what we have done or haven't done.

God's faithfulness does not depend on our faithfulness. The keeping of his promises doesn't depend on the keeping of ours.

So when we pray, we should say something like, "Father in heaven, I call upon you to do for me what you have promised to do. This isn't about me. It's about you. I know I don't deserve this. I'm quite undeserving. But the keeping of your promises depends on your character, not mine. You have promised. You have attached your name to it. It is your reputation that is on the line here. Your character, not mine. So I rejoice that you will indeed keep this promise for me when the time is right. For you are gracious. You are truthful. You are faithful. You are my God."

Then we should relax. We should be still. We should smile. Because we know that the reason we are still waiting for the promise has nothing to do with something we've done wrong or something we haven't done right. God hasn't changed his mind. He hasn't withdrawn his promise.

He *will* keep his promise to you. You can count on it. You can be sure of it. You can be certain of it. Because the keeping of all his promises depends on his character, not yours.

CHAPTER TWO: THE PROMISES CHAPTER

In this chapter I have compiled a list of what I consider to be some of the greatest of God's promises. A brief devotional commentary follows each one.

Now you are certainly welcome to read the entire chapter from beginning to end. However, 50 promises with commentary is a lot to wade through! Actually, I intended this chapter to be a devotional resource that you would come back to frequently after finishing the book. So I suggest that you read the opening section through. Then skim through the 50 Promises section, reading those sections and promises that are meaningful to you at the moment.

In the next few pages I want to briefly describe the types of promises you'll find in the Bible. Then I want to share with you how I use God's promises.

Types of Promises

Attempts to put God's promises into categories are just that—attempts. No categorization can be said to be definitive.

That said, it is generally agreed that God's promises more or less fall into two categories: Conditional promises and unconditional promises. A brief explanation of these types of promises follows next.

Conditional Promises

Conditional promises are promises that can only be kept if the promisee fulfills certain conditions.

A good example of a conditional promise is found in Exodus 19:5. God speaks to the people of Israel, "Now therefore, if you will indeed obey my voice and keep my covenant, you shall be my treasured possession among all peoples, for all the earth is mine."

Notice the "if . . . then" logic. If the people of Israel obey God's commandments, and the covenant he will make with them, then they shall be his treasured possession." The covenant spoken of here was spelled out in the words of the Ten Commandments (Exodus 34:27-28).

Two more examples are found in the fourth chapter of the letter of James: "Draw near to God and he will draw near to you" (4:7) and "Humble yourselves before the Lord, and he will exalt you" (4:9). Both of these show the same "if . . . then" sequence. If you draw near to God, then he will draw near to you. If you humble yourselves before the Lord, then he will exalt you. You have to meet the conditions before God will fulfill the promise.

Not all the conditions in conditional promises are the same, however. In some, the conditions are extremely difficult to fulfill. In others, the opposite is true. Some conditions are so easy as to almost be no condition at all.

A famous story in the Old Testament illustrates this. When poisonous snakes had bit thousands of the people as they were camped out in the wilderness, God told Moses to craft a snake out of bronze and put it on a pole. He then told Moses to give the infected people this promise: Everyone who looked at the Bronze Serpent would be healed. All they had to do was look at it and the promise would be fulfilled. The height of simplicity (Numbers 21:4-9; Jesus refers to this story in John 3:14-15).

The conditions in the promises of prayers are like that. As easy as looking at the bronze snake. So easy as to almost not be conditions at all. All we have to do is ask, or believe, and God will grant our request.

Then there are conditions like the one mentioned previously, in Exodus 19. God promised to make the Israelites his treasured possession, IF they obeyed him: "If you will indeed obey my voice and keep my covenant, then you will be my treasured possession in all the earth." If that sounds easy to you, I'm here to tell you that it wasn't. In fact the rest of the Old Testament shows that the Israelites frequently failed to meet the condition spelled out in that promise—and suffered bitter consequences.

Unconditional Promises

Unconditional promises have no conditions that must be met before the promise can be fulfilled. God's promise to Noah that he would never again flood the entire earth (Genesis 9:11) is a good example. No action on Noah's part, or anyone else's, was necessary.

Another good example is when the Apostle Paul told his readers, "And my God shall supply all your needs according to his riches in Christ Jesus" (Phil 4:19). This is something that God will do, independent of anything we do or don't do.

Implied Promises

It is my view that there is a third kind of promise in the Scriptures. They are not explicit promises per se; but a promise is implied nonetheless. In implied promises something is said about God that is powerfully encouraging and that benefits us greatly.

These implied promises most often point to something that is true about God at any time. But they can also reference past actions of God.

A good example is Isaiah 40:15, 17: "Behold, the nations are like a drop from a bucket, And are regarded as a speck of dust on the scales . . . All the nations are as nothing before Him, They are regarded by Him as less than nothing and meaningless."

These words of Isaiah describe God's power in a memorable way. If entire nations are like a drop in the bucket to him—are less than nothing—then how enormously powerful our God must be. Nothing is promised, but since we know that Isaiah's God is our God, and that he is a God who has promised to use his power to help us, then a promise is implied.

Another good one is recorded in Jeremiah 32:17. Jeremiah exclaims, "Ah, Lord GOD! It is you who have made the heavens and the earth by your great power and by your outstretched arm! Nothing is too hard for you."

Again, nothing explicit is promised in Jeremiah's words. He is simply stating a truth about God. That he created the entire universe by his great power. And that nothing is too hard for him to do.

The clear implication of these words, though, is that because the LORD is also our God, he will exercise that great power for our benefit. That though we will face many problems and situations in our lives that are too hard for us to solve, they will not be too hard for him. That when he makes a promise that to us seems difficult to fulfill, it isn't too difficult for him.

The prophets and apostles sometimes refer to some great work God did in the past in order to encourage those living in the present. These also are implied promises.

The opening words of Psalm 22 are a good example.

"My God, my God, why have you forsaken me? Why are you so far from saving me, from the words of my groaning? [2] O my God, I cry by day, but you do not answer, and by night, but I find no rest. [3] Yet you are holy, enthroned on the praises of Israel. [4] In you our fathers trusted; they trusted, and you delivered them. [5] To you they cried and were rescued; in you they trusted and were not put to shame."

David feels that God has forsaken him. He complains that God has not answered his cry for help. But then he remembers how God delivered the people of God who lived before him when they cried for help. By doing so, he encourages himself. Because he knows that God can and will do the same for him.

There are dozens of these implied promises in the Bible. I'll be referencing some later in the chapter.

How To Use God's Promises

The purpose of this chapter is to give you a healthy sampling of God's promises in order to increase your promises repertoire. I have a hunch that if I randomly stopped Christians on the street and asked them to name three of their favorite promises, many would struggle to comply. And those who were able to name three would probably name the same few.

God has made hundreds of promises and he keeps them all. The more we know and believe, the more we will see fulfilled. It is quite sad when a Christian knows only a few.

Knowing the promises of God is important. But you also have to know how to use them. So I want to recommend to you two very basic ways to use God's promises.

In Prayer

The first way that I use the promises is in prayer. When I have a need or want that one of God's promises speaks to, I have that promise in hand when I pray. It works best if I have the promise written down in front of me. My Bible might be open to the particular promise, for example. That promise, then, becomes the basis of my prayer.

This idea is not new. Christians have used it for centuries.

The Sixteenth Century reformer Martin Luther used God's promises this way. In one of his key writings on prayer, he wrote that when we pray, one of the most necessary things is that "we must have a promise or pledge from God. We must reflect on this promise and remind God of it, and in that way be emboldened to pray with confidence" (Martin Luther, "On Rationtide Prayer and Procession – 1519" AE 42:87).

I agree with Luther. I do the same. Using God's promises in this way enables me to pray with boldness and certainty. It minimizes any doubts I might have. It gives me peace and hope.

I tell God my need or desire. Then I point to the promise and "remind" him of it. I read the promise to him. I tell him, "God, you chose to make this promise. By doing so you have obligated yourself to keep it."

I tell him that it is impossible for him to break any promise, including the one open before me. I call upon him to keep that promise for me. I call upon him to be God for me.

I tell him that because he is the truthful, faithful God, that he must do for me what he has promised. He must do it because he has attached his name and reputation to the promise.

By the way, it is not sin or blasphemy to tell God that we insist that he be the God he has revealed himself to be in the Bible. He said it. He made the promises. So Christians expect him to be who he said he is and do what he said he would do. Otherwise, he is an utterly unknown God. One that can't be trusted. One who shouldn't condemn us when we don't trust him.

It is not sin to demand that he be the truthful, faithful, gracious, loving, generous, powerful, kind, forgiving, saving and promise-keeping God he is. That we won't allow him to excuse his behavior by claiming that he is God and can do as he pleases.

Of course he is God and can do as he pleases. But precisely because he is God, and precisely because he has made promises, those promises constrain and restrict his behavior. They obligate him to do what he has promised and act in ways in keeping with those promises.

In Self-Talk

Psychology has given us important new insights about how what we say to ourselves affects us. How it powerfully shapes our attitudes and moods. How it strongly influences what we believe to be true or not true.

This "self-talk" is all too frequently negative talk. Talk in which we beat ourselves up and tear ourselves down. Talk that is consistently pessimistic. Or talk that convinces us to give up and not even try.

But self-talk is really nothing new. There is a famous example of it in the book of Psalms. But with a pleasant twist.

The author of this particular psalm (Psalm 42) had every reason to engage in negative self-talk. He was an exile in a foreign land among enemies who routinely mocked his God and his faith, saying "Where is your God?" Because of this his "soul was cast down" within him (42:6).

But then in an act of sheer will, he talked back to his despairing thoughts and feelings.

> Why are you cast down, O my soul, and why are you in turmoil within me? Hope in God; for I shall again praise him, my salvation and my God (Psalm 42:11; repeated in Psalm 42:5 and 43:5).

He questioned the legitimacy of his sorrowful thoughts and emotions. He exhorted himself to have hope in God again. He reminded himself that he would again praise his God (because God would help him).

I'm sure you can see where this is going. Self-talk is the second way I use God's promises. I imitate the psalmist in Psalm 42. I talk back to fears I have. I talk back to my doubt. I remind myself what God has promised. And that it is impossible for him to not do what he promised.

I tell myself that no matter how much time has passed, and no matter what has happened in the meantime, what God has promised will happen. That the fulfilling of his promises depends on his character, not mine. It is about him, not me. I tell any doubting thoughts I have where to go (and I often tell them to go to hell).

50 Biblical Promises

Promises of Prayer

We begin with a sampling of promises that pertain to prayer. The ones I've chosen come from the mouth of Jesus himself.

The promises of prayer are, quite simply, awe-inspiring. If you learned and used no other promises than these, your life would be immeasurably enriched.

What all the promises of prayer have in common, of course, is that God promises to give us what we ask.

John 16:23-24

> "Truly, truly, I say to you, whatever you ask of the Father in my name, he will give it to you. 24 Until now you have asked nothing in my name. Ask, and you will receive, that your joy may be full."

Jesus made this promise to his twelve disciples in Jerusalem the night before he was crucified. It is part of a solemn speech Jesus delivered to his intimate circle in the upper room, recorded in John 14-17. The same night as the Last Supper.

In this speech Jesus is preparing his disciples for his death and resurrection, on the one hand, and their role as future leaders in the church, on the other. It contains topics that Jesus considered to be of the utmost importance. Things that were essential for his disciples to know.

The promise begins with the words, "Truly, truly." The expression—uniquely used by Jesus--signals that the saying to follow is solemn and true. It is another way of saying, "I assure you that" or "I solemnly tell you." When you see, "Truly, truly," you know that what follows is important.

What is perhaps the most amazing thing about this promise of prayer is that it is completely open-ended. Jesus says that *whatever* we ask the Father in his name, he will give it to us. He doesn't restrict the requests we make of God in any way. The promise applies to anything we ask God. Not merely some things.

As if saying it once wasn't enough, Jesus repeats the promise in verse 24. His enthusiasm and urgency is unmistakable: "Ask, and you will receive, that your joy may be full!"

By the way, to pray "in Jesus' name" is a way of confessing to God that the only reason he is going to give us what we ask is because of what Jesus has done for us by his atoning death on the cross. He will give us whatever we ask "for Jesus' sake."

Imagine you were trying to have an audience with some world leader. Yet no matter what you said or did you were refused. Now imagine that you had a short note that his son had written for you, saying, "Please grant this person an audience, father. I know him personally and I can vouch for him. Thanks, your son." When the father sees that you came in his son's name, he immediately grants you an audience.

The same thing happens when we come to God the Father in the name of his Son, Jesus. Christ says, "I died for this person, Father. He believes in me and has been baptized. Please grant him an audience."

Mark 11:24

> "Therefore I tell you, whatever you ask in prayer, believe that
> you have received it, and it will be yours."

Like the previous promise, this one in Mark 11:24 is completely
open-ended. The promise applies to *whatever* we might ask God in
prayer. The promise isn't contingent upon what we ask. We can ask
God anything and what we ask will be ours.

Though what we ask doesn't matter, the faith behind the request
does. Remarkably, Jesus tells us that when we make our request of
God, we should believe that we have *already* received it—even though it
may not yet have visibly happened.

How do you "believe that you have received it"? After you make
your request, you thank God for whatever you asked just as you would
if it was right there in front of you as an accomplished fact.

When we do that, Jesus promises that what we asked will be ours.
I'll have more to say about this in Chapter 3.

Matthew 7:7-11

> "Ask, and it will be given to you; seek, and you will find;
> knock, and it will be opened to you. [8] For everyone who asks
> receives, and the one who seeks finds, and to the one who
> knocks it will be opened. 9 Or which one of you, if his son
> asks him for bread, will give him a stone? [10] Or if he asks for a
> fish, will give him a serpent? [11] If you then, who are evil, know
> how to give good gifts to your children, how much more will
> your Father who is in heaven give good things to those who
> ask him!

Jesus made this promise of prayer in his Sermon on the Mount,
recorded in Matthew 5-7. The first words state the promise and set the
tone: "Ask, and it will be given you; seek and you will find; knock and it
will be opened to you." Three quick comments about this.

First, the promises about seeking and knocking aren't additional
promises; they are restating the first promise "Ask, and it will be given
you" for emphasis.

Second, in the original Greek text the three verbs, "ask," "seek," and
"knock," are present imperatives. What this means is that they all have
a durative sense, which, unfortunately, most English translations don't
capture. They should be translated "Be asking, "Be seeking," and "Be
knocking," or even better, "Keep asking," "keep seeking," and "keep

knocking." The way they are usually translated can give the impression that all one has to do is ask, seek or knock once. When, in fact, the promise is, "Keep asking, and eventually you will receive."

Third, this is a command to pray, not just a promise. Jesus isn't merely recommending that we ask, etc. He is commanding us to do so.

Matthew 7:8 again repeats the promises, but with the added detail that the promise is true for anyone no matter who they are. "*Everyone* who asks receives. *The one* who seeks finds. To *the one* who knocks it will be opened."

The final verses are a perfect example of a rhetorical device called the argument from the lesser to the greater. He addresses the parents in the crowd with a series of self-evident questions, in which he essentially says, "If you parents know how to give your kids exactly what they ask ("bread," "fish") rather than something useless or harmful ("stone," "snake") how much more will God, the heavenly Father do so? Are you better than God the Father? Smarter? More loving? More motivated? Hardly! So if you do it and can be counted on to do it, God the Father can be counted on to do it on even more."

Finally, notice that Jesus promises that the Father will give his children "the good things" they ask him. It should be obvious that just as earthly parents will refuse to give their kids the harmful things they ask, so will our Father in heaven.

Matthew 18:19

> "Again I say to you, if two of you agree on earth about anything they ask, it will be done for them by my Father in heaven.

This is a unique promise, because it is a promise that requires that (at least) two Christians are praying. And that they are in agreement in their request.

It is another open-ended promise. The two can be asking God "anything" (Greek: "any matter").

The Greek word translated "earth" can also mean "region," and that is probably the meaning here. Jesus has in mind Christians from the same region or area asking God for the same thing.

Verse 20 adds that they are gathered in Christ's name. So in other words, this promise is set within the context of the gathered church. If you read the preceding verses you will see that this promise in Matthew 18:19 comes in the middle of instruction intended for the gathered church.

Other Promises of Prayer: John 14:13-14; John 15:7; John 15:16; Hebrews 4:15-16; James 5:16b-18; 1 John 5:14-15.

Article: Jesus Wants Us to Pray Our Hearts Out

When I think about everything that Christ says about prayer in the Gospels, I have to ask, "What more could Jesus have done to encourage us to "pray our hearts out"?

Except for what we now call "The Lord's Prayer," Christ's prayer teaching is noteworthy in that he never specifies what we should pray. The focus is always the same. Jesus urges us to ask God for anything we need or want and promises us that God will give us what we ask.

His teaching never gets bogged down in details. He never bothers to hold forth on which requests are appropriate and which aren't. He doesn't seem to be worried at all that his disciples might ask for stupid or selfish things that aren't God's will.

There is nothing in his teaching that even hints at his being afraid that his disciples will abuse his simple promises of prayer, then get discouraged when their errant requests aren't granted. He never addresses that subject.

He could have. On other topics Jesus certainly knew how to articulate nuances. He warned against misunderstandings on other subjects. But he didn't do that when the topic was prayer.

It's as if he didn't want his disciples to even entertain such questions. Because he knew that if he limited the promises of prayer to only a few kinds of requests, it might discourage them from praying.

In fact, have you ever noticed that Jesus never told his disciples that God might say no to their requests? Certainly he knew that this would happen.

We have the example of James and John asking Jesus to let them sit on either side of him in the coming kingdom. We know Christ's response, "It's not mine to give. It is for those for whom it has been prepared" (Mark 10:35-45).

It has always amazed me that when James and John made this request that Jesus didn't use the opportunity to nuance his teaching on prayer. To say something along the lines of, "This is a good opportunity to point out that neither the Father nor I will give you *everything* you ask. God does say, "No," you know. I know I promised you that God will give you whatever you ask in prayer. But *obviously* the Father is not going to give you what you ask unless it is something that is God's will, or something you actually need—not just something you want. Obviously the Father will only give you what you ask if it glorifies God and furthers his kingdom, or if it is spiritual, or if it comes from pure and unselfish motives, etc."

But he didn't do this. Jesus never qualified his teaching on prayer in this way. He never tried to anticipate misuses of his promises. Never restricted his promises to certain kinds of Christians or certain levels of sanctification.

Why not? Because, as I said, Jesus didn't want to discourage us in any way from praying our hearts out. He didn't want to discourage us from asking God whatever it is we think we or someone else needs; and from having the assurance that when we do, God will give it.

Promises of Provision

These are promises in which God pledges to provide for us. He promises to provide all the things we need to live in this world. Food. Shelter. Employment. Income. Friendship. Companionship. Love. And much more besides.

Psalm 145:15-16

"The eyes of all look to you, and you give them their food in due season. [16] You open your hand; you satisfy the desire of every living thing."

It is from God's hand that all that satisfies comes. I love this promise because it states that God satisfies. That is no small thing. Since most of us are hard to satisfy and aren't satisfied for long.

I also love it because it tells us that God satisfies "the desire" of every living thing. What we "want" and not just what we "need."

We should come before God with this promise in hand and pray, "God, it is written that you open your hand and satisfy the desire of every living thing. So I call upon you to keep this promise for me. Be the God that this passage says you are—for me. Satisfy me. Satisfy my desires and provide for me!"

Psalm 34:10

"The young lions suffer want and hunger; but those who seek the LORD lack no good thing."

Lions were the most effective hunters in David's world. It was rare that they didn't find and bring down prey. They were tenacious, resourceful and proactive. They went out and got what they wanted and made it happen. However, even these "go-getters" had times of want and hunger.

Those who seek the LORD are promised that they will fare better than such "movers and shakers." In fact, they will lack "no good thing," not just food. The Hebrew word translated "seek" here means to make supplication to God with prayers and demands.

So when your current circumstances appear to give lie to this promise, then go before God with this promise in hand, and "remind" him of it. Humbly insist that he keep this promise for you.

Psalm 55:22

"Cast your burden on the LORD, and he will sustain you; he will never permit the righteous to be moved."

The imagery here is that of carrying a heavy load on one's back.

We all know what a burden is. Some problem or heartache we are carrying that weighs us down. That is perhaps so heavy that it is painful or exhausting to carry. Or is crushing the life out of us. A relationship gone bad. Sickness or injury. A micromanaging boss. Bills to pay and nothing to pay them with. A loved one in trouble. Or some personal failure that has filled us with self-doubt.

If we were to literally "cast" or "throw" our burden on the LORD, he would carry it instead of us. So to cast our burden on the LORD means to trust him to do just that. To trust him to solve our problem. To "let go and let God."

The promise is that when you do, "he will sustain you." The particular form of the Hebrew verb translated "sustain" actually means to "provide." Or to "provide sustenance." So it is a promise that God will remove our burden and solve our problem by providing whatever we are lacking, especially material things.

Matthew 6:31

"Therefore do not be anxious, saying, 'What shall we eat?' or 'What shall we drink?' or 'What shall we wear?' 32 For the

Gentiles seek after all these things, and your heavenly Father knows that you need them all. [33] But seek first the kingdom of God and his righteousness, and all these things will be added to you."

When we are lacking the things we need to live in this world, the easiest thing to do is worry. It can be frightening to face unemployment, eviction, poverty or homelessness--or even the threat of these things. Yet, Jesus tells us not to worry. He tells us not to worry because he knew for certain that God will always provide for his children.

He says, "The Gentiles seek after all these things." "Gentiles" in this context means "unbelievers." His point is, first, "Why would you worry like the Gentiles do? You are believers. You are God's own children!" And second, "Your heavenly Father knows that you need them all and will most certainly give them to you."

Last comes the promise, which is a conditional one. "Seek first God's kingdom and righteousness, and all these things will be added to you." To "seek . . . God's kingdom and righteousness" means to "strive" or "earnestly desire" to be a member of God's kingdom.

To seek "first," speaks to priority. It means to care more about making sure that you are in good standing with God (by believing that Christ Jesus died for you) than you do about having the things of the world—even necessary things. Which, if you are a Christian, you are striving to do already.

You don't have to do this perfectly. None of us ever perfectly seeks "first" God's kingdom.

Do this, and God will provide food, water, clothing, and whatever else you need for this life: "All these things will be added to you."

Romans 8:32

"He who did not spare his own Son but gave him up for us all, how will he not also with him graciously give us all things?"

This extraordinary promise, written by the Apostle Paul, is couched in a rhetorical flourish called the argument from the greater to the lesser.

If God didn't hold back, but was willing to give his own Son over to death for us and our salvation—which was the greatest gift he could possibly give—will he hold back and not give us all the lesser things we need?

If he was so committed to us in love, so intent on providing for us, that he refused to spare his Son from all the suffering of the cross—which was the hardest thing God ever did—won't he also give us everything else we need, which are mere trifles by comparison? Of course he will!

Two words deserve comment. Paul writes that God will *graciously* give us *all* things. "Graciously" means that God will give us all things freely, whether we "deserve" them or not. Our performance or behavior or worthiness has nothing to do with it. "All things" means whatever we lack, no matter what it is, or whether we realize it or not. Nothing is exempted or excluded.

The promise is that God will provide every conceivable thing we could possibly need.

Philippians 4:19

"And my God will supply every need of yours according to his riches in glory in Christ Jesus."

As mentioned earlier, this is a beautiful example of an unconditional promise. The promise isn't dependent upon anything we do, or have to do. God will do what is promised here for no other reason than that he has pledged himself to do so.

What is promised here is awesome. God will take from his infinite and divine storehouse of riches and will fully supply *any and every* need you could conceivably have.

Other Promises of Provision: Psalm 23:1; Psalm 103:5; Psalm 81:10; Psalm 107:9; 1 Timothy 6:17.

Article: Needs and Wants

I have often heard people say, "God never promised to give us what we want, just what we need." But is it true?

First of all, what is a *need*? Some are quick to insist that a need is always and only a "necessity." Something that is absolutely necessary to live in this world. Food. Water. Clothing. Not much more.

But in most languages there is a wide range of meanings for the word "need." The word can and does mean far more than basic necessities. This is certainly true of the Biblical words (Hebrew and Greek) that are translated "need."

In fact, do a simple concordance study on the word "need" and you will see what I mean. There is nothing in the word "need" that requires it to mean "what is absolutely necessary to live."

A good working definition, then, is that a need is something that is lacking for some purpose or end. Something that is lacking so that a person can live. Something that is lacking so that a person can be happy. Something that is lacking so that a person can be successful. Just to name a few examples.

Even if it could be proven that "need" always means the most basic necessities, who decides what those basic necessities are? Are basic necessities things without which a person would die? Things upon which biological life depends? Is this the Biblical definition?

According to Jesus in Luke 10, "only one thing is needed": Listening to God's Word (10:42). This reflects the Old Testament teaching that man does not live by bread alone but by every word of God (Deuteronomy 8:3; Jesus quotes this in Matthew 4:4). His point is that if we really want to get down to what is *absolutely* necessary for life, God's Word is it.

Therefore—since the word "need" doesn't always or only mean "necessity" linguistically, and "necessity" is so obviously open to interpretation depending on context and each person's current life situation—it is wrong to insist that it only means what we must have to support biological life. Such as food, water and shelter.

For example, when St. Paul wrote to the Philippians, "And my God shall supply all your needs according to his riches in Christ Jesus (4:19)," we are wrongly restricting the passage if we assume that "needs" are only the most basic necessities. Paul doesn't restrict it and neither should we.

The second and related question is, "What is a want?" Like "need," the word "want" is open to interpretation according to each person's life situation. Neither is there any silver-bullet Biblical definition that can help us.

There is just no getting around the fact that the line between want and need is blurry.

Also, the Bible never states anywhere that God promises to give us what we need, but not what we want. Actually, he promises to give us what we want, too! "Delight yourself in the LORD and he will give you the desires of your heart" (Psalm 37:4). "If you abide in me, and my words abide in you, ask whatever you wish, and it will be done for you" (John 15:7).

So what conclusions can we reach?

First, the Bible never makes a fixed distinction between needs and wants. Second, we shouldn't be so quick to conclude that the thing we are praying about isn't a need, simply because it isn't an absolute necessity. Nor should we— and this is absolutely crucial--ever restrict the many promises of provision to bare necessities only. As if those promises only promise bare necessities.

Promises of Rescue from Trouble

Psalm 50:15

"and call upon me in the day of trouble; I will deliver you, and you shall glorify me."

This promise is so clear that it barely needs explanation. It is a promise that God will rescue those who are experiencing a "day of trouble."

The Hebrew word for trouble in this verse is a common one. It is a word that describes any kind of distress. In the Bible it is used for great distresses, such as a city besieged by an enemy army. But it also used for lesser troubles.

No one should ever fail to call upon God because they think their trouble isn't serious enough. Or that God might not even consider it to be legitimate trouble. If it is trouble to you, it is trouble to him.

Those experiencing a time of trouble are to "call upon" God. Interestingly, the particular Hebrew word used here always refers to speech that is out loud. So it might be better to understand it as "call out" to God.

God promises to rescue the one who calls to him in trouble. God also knows that when the rescue comes the rescued one will indeed honor him as "the Mighty One, God the LORD" (50:1).

One last thought. The context of this promise is important. When one reads all of Psalm 50, one sees that the psalm records God's loving rebuke of his people. He tells them that what he is really looking for from them is not a sacrifice of animals, but a sacrifice of thanksgiving (50:14).

Psalm 34:17-19

"When the righteous cry for help, the LORD hears and delivers them out of all their troubles. [18] The LORD is near to the brokenhearted and saves the crushed in spirit. [19] Many are the afflictions of the righteous, but the LORD delivers him out of them all."

This passage actually contains three promises, each having to do with God delivering us from our troubles.

The first is, "When the righteous cry for help, the LORD hears and delivers them out of all their troubles."

This is a promise that applies to "the righteous." People that David often contrasts with "the wicked." So who are the righteous?

They are people who are "right with God." People who God regards as innocent of wrongdoing. People who he regards as having kept his commandments.

According to the New Testament, a person is declared righteous (justified) by faith in Jesus Christ who atoned for all their sins on the cross. When they believe in Jesus, God no longer considers their sins but considers them righteous. So righteous = Christian.

As in Psalm 50:15, the Hebrew verb translated "cry" means to cry out loud. Notice that the promise is that God will deliver them from ALL their troubles.

The second promise is, "The LORD is near to the brokenhearted and saves the crushed in spirit (v. 18)."

It is not only from dangerous or threatening situations that we need to be rescued. Sometimes we need to be saved from emotional or mental distress.

The first thing this touching promise tells us is that "the LORD is near to the brokenhearted." The "brokenhearted" is someone who is filled with profound sadness for nearly any reason. Rejection. Betrayal. Loss of a loved one. Failure. Disappointment. Guilt over one's sinfulness. Any of these things can create a broken heart (Psalm 51:19). Whatever the reason, if your heart is broken, the LORD is "near" you—as close as he can be—even though you may feel totally alone in your sadness.

But God doesn't stop there. This passage also promises us that God "saves the crushed in spirit." The Hebrew word for "crushed" can mean "dust," and appears, for example, in Genesis 3:15, "For you are dust and to dust you shall return." But "the crushed in spirit" refers to someone who has been humiliated, is despairing, or has been reduced to nothing. Such a one will most certainly be rescued by God.

The third promise is, "Many are the afflictions of the righteous, but the LORD delivers him out of them all" (34:19).

Believers in Christ do not escape afflictions. Throughout their lives they will have them. The word translated "afflictions" is one that can mean "deprivation," "calamity" or "misfortune." The afflictions can be the result of evil in the world, or the result of our own foolish decisions.

Regardless of the cause of afflictions, God's Word promises us that "The LORD delivers him out of them all." God eventually rescues us from all our afflictions so that our suffering ends.

Isaiah 46:4

"Even to your old age I am he, and to gray hairs I will carry you. I have made, and I will bear; I will carry and will save."

I love this promise. God made this promise to the people of Judah after they had been taken captive to Babylon. They definitely needed rescue.

This same moving promise applies to any among God's people who need rescue.

"Even to your old age I am he, and to gray hairs, I will carry you." Translation: "Even when you are old, to the very end of your life, I will lovingly carry you as I did when you were a little child, as a parent carries a toddler.

"I will carry and will save." You now find yourself in captivity. But I will pick you up. I will carry you to safety and freedom. I will deliver you from your captivity.

Other Promises of Rescue: Psalm 62:1; Psalm 68:20; Psalm 91:15; Psalm 145:19.

Promises of Strength

We all need strength. We need to be strengthened spiritually, emotionally, physically and mentally. We need strength to face a crisis. Strength to face another day. Or maybe strength to step outside of our comfort zone to do something we know we must do. Here are several verses in which God promises to give us strength.

Isaiah 40:29-31

"He gives power to the faint, and to him who has no might he increases strength. [30] Even youths shall faint and be weary, and young men shall fall exhausted; [31] but they who wait for the LORD shall renew their strength; they shall mount up with wings like eagles; they shall run and not be weary; they shall walk and not faint."

God makes this promise to the one who is "faint." The Hebrew word used refers to those who are faint because of lack of food or water as they travel through the desert; but it can refer to any kind of weariness.

So the promise applies to one who is worn out or worn down. To one who is depleted or drained. It is made to one whose reserves are spent. Or to one who is beaten down or burnt out. It is a promise to the one who is weary to the bone, whose will is sapped, or who has no fight left.

God promises to increase strength for the one who has no might. Which means he promises to strengthen their resolve, to renew their zeal, to fortify their wills and to increase their energy. So that they can take up the struggle again, face down the problem, or do the work that needs doing.

Even the young—the strongest among us—grow weary and collapse. But Isaiah promises that they who wait for the LORD, shall renew their strength. Though they previously struggled to take just one more step, when God revitalizes them they will be like eagles taking flight. From laying collapsed on the track of life, they will be strengthened to stand up again and walk. They will be energized to run.

To wait for the LORD means to wait for him to keep his promise to us. So 40:31 is saying that those who are waiting for what God promised to happen, will gain new strength—even before what God promised happens.

Isaiah 41:10

"Fear not, for I am with you; be not dismayed, for I am your God; I will strengthen you, I will help you, I will uphold you with my righteous right hand."

What drains our strength? Far more than physical exertion. In this passage God targets an emotion that has the potential to drain and deplete our strength quicker than almost anything else: Fear.

When fear grabs hold of a person, it can change him from being strong to being weak in an instant. Fear sucks the life out of us, robbing us of our courage, our fortitude, our perseverance and our willingness to fight the good fight. It turns a person of perpetual motion into a limp and motionless rag.

So God knows what he is doing when he promises strength as an antidote to fear. "Fear not, I am with you . . . I will strengthen you . . . I will hold you up with my righteous right hand." I like that last line. It's as if God is saying, "I know your knees are buckling from fear, but I will hold you up so that you won't collapse." Be strengthened!

1 Peter 5:10-11

> And after you have suffered a little while, the God of all grace,
> who has called you to his eternal glory in Christ, will himself
> restore, confirm, strengthen, and establish you.

When we are suffering, one of the worst things about it is that it seems like it will never end.

This promise is a needed reminder that—whatever the pain and whatever the hardship—God never lets it go on without end. In his mercy he will end it, after we have suffered a "little while."

Peter gave this sweet promise of hope to Christians who were being attacked by the devil in some way, perhaps through persecution (5:8-9). He promises them that the God of all grace will come to them in their suffering and strengthen them.

To emphasize just how completely God will strengthen them, the apostle piles on the verbs, saying it four different ways. God himself will:

- "restore" – This Greek verb means to put something in order so that it functions well. To fix something that is broken.
- "confirm" – This verb means to be made inwardly firm or committed.
- "strengthen" – This Greek verb appears only here in the New Testament.
- "establish" – The word means to lay a foundation. To ground.

Be sure to notice how Peter describes who this God is who will strengthen them. He is "the God of all grace, who has called you to his eternal glory in Christ."

When we are going through any kind of prolonged suffering it is so easy to buy into the temptation that God is "smiting" us for some reason.

But that, says Peter, is not who he is. He is the God of all grace, a

God whose whole attitude toward us is one of grace—undeserved favor, kindness and tenderness. He is the God who has given us eternal glory in Christ. That's the kind of loving and generous and forgiving God he always is, no matter what is going on in our lives.

Promises of Direction

There are so many people who feel lost today. There is a whole world before them. But they have no idea what to do with it. Or what their place is in it. They don't know what they're supposed to do with their lives. Or what their purpose is.

There are so many people who long for direction. They long for direction in the little decisions. And they long for direction for the big life issues. The kind of education they should pursue. The kind of work they should do. Who they should date or marry. Whether they should marry. Where they should live.

The good news is that God understands people who need direction. He agrees with what the prophet Jeremiah once said: "I know, O LORD, that the way of man is not in himself, that it is not in man who walks to direct his steps" (Jeremiah 10:23). And he promises to direct you.

So whether you are one of those who feel lost, or are just in need of God's direction, here are promises that will help.

Psalm 25:12

> "Who are they that fear the LORD? He will teach them the
> way that they should choose."

"Those who fear the LORD" is another way of saying "those whose God is the LORD." To such people it is promised that God will direct them in their choices; he will show them the way to go.

How that direction will happen isn't specified. Because God can do so in so many different ways. But we are promised that he will give us the direction we need.

Isaiah 50:10

> Who among you fears the LORD and obeys the voice of his
> servant? Let him who walks in darkness and has no light trust
> in the name of the LORD and rely on his God.

Several chapters in Isaiah make reference to the God's "Servant." "The Servant" is another name for the promised Messiah or Christ. Isaiah tells us that the promise is for "those whose God is the LORD and who obey the voice of the Messiah"—another way of saying "Christian."

More specifically it is for someone "who walks in darkness and has no light." Which is a perfect description of someone who is lost and doesn't know which way to go; who desperately needs direction. The implied promise is that when such "lost in the dark" ones trust in the LORD and rely on their God, God will give them the "light" they need to find their way.

Promises of Inner Peace

Something essential to our wellbeing is inner peace. Peace of mind. Unfortunately, inner peace is frustratingly elusive. So difficult to attain. So easy to lose. So it is good news that God promises to give it to us.

John 14:27

> "Peace I leave with you; my peace I give to you. Not as the world gives do I give to you. Let not your hearts be troubled, neither let them be afraid."

It was the night before he died. Jesus had been telling his disciples that he was going to leave them. He was going to return to the Father. He saw the looks on their faces. He knew what they were feeling. What he told them had filled them with inner turmoil. They were worried. They were afraid. It was to give them peace right then and there that Jesus spoke this beautiful promise.

There are so many, many emotions that dislodge and replace our peace of mind. Worry. Fear. Hate. Discontentment. Hurt. Envy. Jealousy. Self-doubt. Even love can evict peace from our hearts.

And there are so many, many circumstances we experience that make those negative emotional states easy to fall into. Demands at work or school. Conflict with people. Illness. Injury. The inability to find direction in our lives. Loss of love. Loss of job. Loss of property or possessions. Failure to meet someone's expectations. Being the constant target of criticism, gossip or abuse. Death of a loved one. The list is long.

If peace has been dislodged from your heart for any reason, then Jesus speaks this promise to you. "Peace, I leave with you. My peace I give you. . . Let not your heart be troubled. Neither let it be afraid." The words of Jesus powerfully convey what they say.

Philippians 4:6-7

"Do not be anxious about anything, but in everything by prayer and supplication with thanksgiving let your requests be made known to God. [7] And the peace of God, which surpasses all understanding, will guard your hearts and your minds in Christ Jesus."

This is a promise of peace and prayer rolled into one.

The Apostle Paul targets the problem of worry, that wretched robber emotion that steals our peace. His basic message is that when we find ourselves beginning to worry, we should stop and immediately pray. We should ask God for whatever it is we need or want.

When we do so—not only will God grant our request—we are promised that the peace of God will guard our hearts and minds. In memorable language, Paul personifies God's peace as a guard or sentry standing watch over our emotions and thoughts, refusing entry to worry or anything else that might rob us of peace.

The next time you feel yourself slipping into worry, use this promise. Let your requests be known to God. Thank him for your life as it is. God will not only give his peace. But that peace will protect and guard your emotions and thoughts from all that might disturb you.

Promises of Prosperity

Biblically speaking, "prosperity" can refer to any kind of bounty. Promises of prosperity aren't necessarily about financial prosperity—as the very first promise below will make clear.

Luke 6:38

"Give, and it will be given to you. Good measure, pressed down, shaken together, running over, will be put into your lap. For with the measure you use it will be measured back to you."

Right up front I want you to notice that money isn't mentioned. This promise is that when we give, it will be given back to us. Christ leaves the thing given undefined. It could be anything positive we give. Love . . . forgiveness . . . mercy . . . time . . . a listening ear . . . asked for advice . . . free labor . . . charitable giving . . . or something else.

When we give, Jesus promises that it will be given to us, "good measure, pressed down, shaken together, running over, will be put into your lap."

The imagery here is that of dry goods being poured into a bushel basket. An easy way to shortchange someone was to pour something in a basket and not press it down or shake the product. Pressing it down and shaking it together assured the buyer that the bushel was truly full.

So picture someone with a bushel on their lap. The one giving pours "a good measure" (generously) of the product into the bushel. He then presses it down and shakes it to assure that the bushel is full. But he's not done. He starts pouring again and the bushel overflows into his lap. A beautiful way to picture someone getting more than they should have, more than they were expecting. It is a picture of lavish generosity.

What Jesus also leaves open is that what we are given back might not be exactly what we gave. Neither is there any suggestion that we will be given back something immediately.

He ends the promise with a proverbial saying, not unique to Christianity: "By the measure you measure, it will be measured to you in return." Which means, "The measure you give will be the measure you get. So if you give generously it will be given back to you generously.

Proverbs 19:17

"Whoever is generous to the poor lends to the LORD, and he will repay him for his deed."

Here is a very specific promise that emphasizes how God views showing generosity to the poor. God identifies so closely with them that to lend to the poor is to lend to God. The person who does so is promised that God will repay him for his deed.

When in doubt about whether the person in question is truly "poor," give anyway.

2 Corinthians 9:6

"The point is this: whoever sows sparingly will also reap sparingly, and whoever sows bountifully will also reap bountifully."

Here is what is often called the "law" of sowing and reaping. But it really is a promise. We really do reap what we sow in the realm of giving. When we sow bountifully, God sees to it that we reap bountifully.

In this section of his second letter to the Christians in Corinth, Paul was discussing a financial contribution that the Corinthians had promised to give, but hadn't yet given. It is within that context that he wrote about sowing and reaping.

2 Corinthians 9:8

> "And God is able to provide you with every blessing in abundance, so that by always having enough of everything, you may share abundantly in every good work" (NRS).

This is a continuation of the Apostle's discussion of giving in his second letter to the Christians at Corinth. He touches upon a common excuse for not giving.

What often keeps people from giving, or giving more, is their belief that they don't have enough for themselves. So how can they give to others? Some call this a mindset of scarcity.

Paul speaks to this mindset, offering this word of assurance, which is really an implied promise of provision. In a way he is saying, "God's got you covered. You don't have to worry about not having enough and running out. He is more than able to ensure that you always have enough of everything so that you can give generously to others.

Promises of Comfort

It is when we are hurting or sad that the need for comfort arises. Picture a mother holding her little one close, stroking her hair, kissing wherever the hurt is. That's comfort. Comfort dries our tears and makes us feel better. It lessens the pain. It cheers us up.

God brings the promised comfort to us in more than one way. He does it through a person who comforts us . . . through something that happens to us . . . or through something that we think or hear or read, such as God's Word. Just to name a few.

Isaiah 66:13

> "As one whom his mother comforts, so I will comfort you."

God holds before our eyes the beautiful picture of a mother comforting her child. Regardless of our ethnicity or culture, everyone understands this picture. Everyone understands that mothers are dispensers of the sweetest comfort. That they have the power to dry our tears and make us feel better by their hugs and kisses, and by their caresses and tender words.

God has that power too. He promises us that he will comfort us like a mother comforts her child. That he will lift us up on his lap and hold us. That he will wipe our tears away and "make it all better."

Comfort isn't always easy to describe or explain. But we know it when we feel it.

Matthew 5:4

"Blessed are those who mourn, for they shall be comforted."

This is the second of the nine beatitudes Jesus spoke at the very beginning of his Sermon on the Mount. Each of the beatitudes describes as "blessed" people in particular emotional states (1-3), people who do certain things (4-7), or people in certain settings (8-9). Each one tells us why these people are blessed. In all of the beatitudes Jesus calls people blessed that conventional wisdom calls wretched. He turns the normal way of evaluating upside down.

What is often overlooked is that this second beatitude is a beautiful promise. Jesus promises that those who mourn will be comforted.

In English, the word "mourn" is almost always taken to mean the grieving that accompanies death. But the Greek word translated "mourn" can mean any kind of grieving or sadness. It isn't limited to the context of death.

Even in English the word "mourn" can describe people grieving over any kind of loss. People can mourn the loss of employment . . . the loss of a friend who moved away . . . the loss of property . . . the loss of health . . . the loss of the full use of our bodies or minds . . . The loss of youth and vitality . . . or the loss of freedom.

So if you are feeling sad right now, or are grieving over any loss, Jesus makes this promise to you. He assures you that you will be comforted.

2 Corinthians 1:3-4

"Blessed be the God and Father of our Lord Jesus Christ, the Father of mercies and God of all comfort, [4] who comforts us in all our affliction, so that we may be able to comfort those who are in any affliction, with the comfort with which we ourselves are comforted by God."

This passage makes two statements about God that are implied promises. First, Paul calls God, the "God of all comfort." It is who he is. He is the source and cause of all true comfort. Second, the apostle says that this God "comforts us in our troubles." It is what he does. It is what he always does.

Then Paul goes on to say that when God keeps his promise of comfort to us, it has the added purpose of making us the comforters of others. We take the comfort he has provided us in our troubles and share it with others in their troubles.

Promises of Forgiveness

To be forgiven when we have wronged someone is nothing less than liberation. To be forgiven is to be set free. From guilt. Or shame. Or a tormented conscience.

It is also reconciliation. When we are forgiven by someone, we are reconciled to that person. No longer separated from them. Once forgiven, the rupture is healed. We are back in their good graces.

No compilation of God's promises would be complete without promises of forgiveness. The Bible is chock-full of them. Forgiveness is the heart and soul of the Christian faith. One of the core teachings of the Bible.

Its message is that all have sinned. Our sins have separated us from God. But because he loved us and refused to give us up, God fully forgave us of all sins through the atoning death of Jesus Christ. By forgiving us we were reconciled to him. All who believe that he died for them make that forgiveness their own.

The purpose of guilt is to show us our need for forgiveness. However, when you feel guilty, the first thing you should ascertain is whether it is true or false guilt. False guilt means feeling guilty even though you've done nothing wrong. Some people are prone to feeling guilty. They can be victimized by people who are good at making others feel guilty. So be aware of that.

If, however, you are feeling guilty because you know you've done something wrong, then the first thing you should do is confess your sin; and then believe the Gospel: That because Jesus died for you on the cross, God has forgiven you. If, having confessed your sins and believed the Gospel, your guilt feelings remain or return, don't allow those feelings to deceive you into thinking you are not forgiven. Feeling guilty after you have confessed your sin and believed the Gospel is also false guilt.

John 1:29

> The next day John the Baptist saw Jesus coming toward him, and said, "Behold, the Lamb of God, who takes away the sin of the world!

This passage concisely and clearly defines the source of all forgiveness. It is Jesus, and Jesus alone, who took away the sin of the world. And he did so by being the sacrificial lamb of God when he died on the cross. Jesus is the reason that forgiveness can be offered to us. His sacrificial death on the cross is the wellspring from which all forgiveness comes.

What I find so comforting about this promise though, is that it informs us that the Lamb of God takes away "the sin of the *world*." That means every sin that was ever committed or that ever will be committed, by anyone in the world, from beginning to end. It includes anything wrong we have done or might do, no matter what it is. Whether the sin is known to us or unknown . . . hidden or public . . . large or small . . . mortal or venial . . . intentional or unintentional. Whether it broke God's law or man's.

Acts 10:43

"To him all the prophets bear witness that everyone who believes in him receives forgiveness of sins through his name."

A beautiful statement that promises us that when we believe in Jesus we receive forgiveness of sins. Faith is how we receive God's forgiveness; how we make the forgiveness that Christ won on the cross our own. When I believe that he died for *my* sins, I am forgiven of my sins.

Acts 2:38

And Peter said to them, "Repent and be baptized every one of you in the name of Jesus Christ for the forgiveness of your sins.

This promise is important because it tells us that we need to repent of our sins. Which means that we have to confess that we *have* sinned, intend to turn away from it, and then believe that through Christ's death our sins are forgiven.

It's also important because it tells us that the forgiveness of our sins also comes through baptism. The source of our forgiveness is Christ's death on the cross. But God also established a delivery system to get that forgiveness to all people. His word (both the preached and written words of God), baptism and the Lord's Supper is that delivery system.

1 John 1:9

If we confess our sins, he is faithful and just to forgive us our sins and to cleanse us from all unrighteousness.

Here we are promised that God will forgive us if we confess our sins. See my explanation after the Acts 2:38 promise above.

Isaiah 43:25

"I, I am he who blots out your transgressions for my own
sake, and I will not remember your sins.

God makes an amazing promise: That not only will he blot out our
transgressions by his grace (grace = "for my own sake")—but he will
also no longer remember our sins. This promise is repeated in Jeremiah
31 and Hebrews 8 and 10.

So if after we have already confessed our sin and been forgiven, we
continued to tell God how sorry we were for that sin, if God chose to
speak to us, he would say, "I have no memory of that. I have no idea
what you're talking about."

Of course, when it comes to forgiving, there is one obvious
difference between God and us. When God forgives, he forgets. When
we forgive—in most cases—we can't ever fully forget. But that doesn't
mean we haven't truly forgiven.

Promises of Eternal Life

There are promises and there are *promises*. Along with the promises
of forgiveness and salvation, the greatest of all of God's promises is the
promise of eternal life. It is *the* promise: "And this is the promise that
he made to us: eternal life" (1 John 2:25). We are promised that a
glorious eternal life with God awaits us after we die.

There are many, many promises of eternal life in the Bible. Here are
two of the best known.

John 3:16

"For God so loved the world, that he gave his only Son, that
whoever believes in him shall not perish but have eternal life.

John 3:16, arguably the best known verse in the Bible, is also a
promise of eternal life. The promise is in the second half of the verse:
"whoever believes in him (God's Son) shall not perish but have eternal
life."

But before God could offer us eternal life, he first "gave his only
Son." Which means he gave him to become one of us. Jesus Christ is
God incarnate. "But when the fullness of time had come, God sent
forth his Son, born of woman" (Galatians 4:4). It means he gave him to
be crucified. "In this is love, not that we loved God but that he loved
us and sent his Son to be the atoning sacrifice for our sins" (1 John

4:10). On the cross, "Christ also suffered once for sins, the righteous for the unrighteous, that he might bring us to God" (1 Peter 3:18).

The promise is that whoever believes in the Son--that he is the one God gave to be the atoning sacrifice for our sins--will have eternal life.

John 6:40

> "For this is the will of my Father, that everyone who looks on the Son and believes in him may have eternal life, and I will raise him up on the last day."

Though similar to John 3:16, this saying of Jesus also says that on the last day he will raise up everyone who believes in him. He further says that this promise is the will of his Father.

The Bible teaches in many places that when Christ returns on the last day, that all those who believed in him will be raised from the dead just before being taken up to heaven. They will be raised with bodies that are without sin and that will never die.

Later in the Gospel of John, Jesus touches on the same theme in his famous words to Martha: "Jesus said to her, "I am the resurrection and the life. Whoever believes in me, though he die, yet shall he live, [26] and everyone who lives and believes in me shall never die" (11:25-26).

About that last day, St. Paul wrote, "Behold! I tell you a mystery . . . we shall all be changed, [52] in a moment, in the twinkling of an eye, at the last trumpet. For the trumpet will sound, and the dead will be raised imperishable, and we shall be changed. For this perishable body must put on the imperishable, and this mortal body must put on immortality" (1 Corinthians 15:51-53).

Promises of Protection

There are many promises of protection in the Scriptures. Why so many? Because the people who wrote them, such as David or the first Christians, were often in grave danger. They had enemies who were literally trying to kill or imprison them.

But you don't have to be facing such life-threatening dangers to use and benefit from the promises of protection. Every single day each of us encounter people and things that can harm us: Potential accidents, injury, sickness, wicked weather, or the ruin of our reputations.

Psalm 9:9-10

> The LORD is a stronghold for the oppressed, a stronghold in times of trouble. [10] And those who know your name put their

trust in you, for you, O LORD, have not forsaken those who seek you.

In the ancient world, the ultimate place of safety or protection was some place high in the mountains that was inaccessible to enemies. It was variously called a "refuge," "stronghold," or "secure height." So it is fitting that the psalmists compare God to such a stronghold. Because he was for them the ultimate protection and safety.

In Psalm 9:9-10, we are told that the LORD is a stronghold for the oppressed. And a stronghold in times of trouble.

Those who know God gladly trust him to protect them: "those who know your name put their trust in you, for you LORD, have not forsaken those who seek you."

Psalm 31:20

In the cover of your presence you hide them from the plots of men; you store them in your shelter from the strife of tongues.

The paranoid person thinks that everyone is out to get them. But sometimes we actually do have someone who is plotting against us, to harm or ruin us. This passage reminds us that those who trust God are hidden from the plots of men in the secret place of his presence. God not only gives them shelter but is their shelter from the ugly falsehoods that others are saying about them.

Proverbs 18:10

"The name of the LORD is a strong tower; the righteous man runs into it and is safe."

Another place that was a place of protection in the ancient world was a tower. It was a place that a person in danger could run into to be safe. In a much greater way, "the name of the LORD" is a fortified tower that we can run into to be safe from any or all dangers.

Isaiah 43:1-3

"Fear not, for I have redeemed you; I have called you by name, you are mine. ^{2} When you pass through the waters, I will be with you; and through the rivers, they shall not overwhelm you; when you walk through fire you shall not be burned, and the flame shall not consume you. ^{3} For I am the LORD your God, the Holy One of Israel, your Savior."

These words of God in Isaiah 43 express one of the most hope-inspiring promises in the Bible.

God speaks to those who are terribly afraid. Afraid of some impending threat. The threat pictured here is flood waters, a raging river and a chaotic wildfire, all of which were and are potentially deadly dangers.

First, he reminds us who we are. We are those whom he has redeemed. He paid a costly ransom to set us free from our captivity. That ransom was the blood of Christ shed in death on the cross (1 Peter 1:18). That's how beloved we are to him. He is the one who named us. We are his, members of his intimate family. Given this, isn't it obvious that he will protect us?

So when you are "passing through the waters . . . and through the rivers", that is, when you are facing some terrifying situation that threatens to engulf and overwhelm you, "he will be with you . . . and they will not sweep you away or drown you." You will be protected from all harm! When you are "walking through fire . . . and the flame" "you shall not be burned . . . or consumed." You will be protected from all harm. Why would God do this for you? Because he is the LORD, your God, your Savior.

Romans 8:31

"If God is for us, who can be against us?"

If *God* is for us, who can be against us? If the omnipotent Creator is for us, who is over all, who or what can possibly be against us so as to harm us?

If God is *for* us, who can be against us? If God loves us, has pledged himself to us, is on our side and in our corner, then who or what can possibly lay a finger on us?

Other Promises of Protection: Psalm 46:1; Psalm 62:8; Psalm 118:6; Psalm 125:2; Isaiah 25:4; 2 Thessalonians 3:3.

Other Promises

This last section contains a sampling of other promises that don't necessarily fit comfortably into any one category.

Romans 8:28

"And we know that for those who love God all things work together for good, for those who are called according to his purpose."

This promise applies to every believer. No matter what the specific situation may be, it offers hope to everyone. The promise is that "all things work together for good."

The Apostle Paul isn't saying, "It will all work out." Or "Everything happens for a reason."

He is saying that that in every situation or circumstance we find ourselves, God so orchestrates events that it all turns out for our good. Even when our current circumstances are terrible. Especially when our current circumstances are terrible.

Did you notice that Paul begins his statement with the words, "And we know"? He assumes that the Christians in Rome to whom he is writing know what he writes in Romans 8:28. As if it was some kind of self-evident truth. Why did he assume that they knew already? I think it was because of two well-known examples.

First, the Roman Christians knew what had happened to Jesus. How on the third day after being appallingly crucified he was raised from the dead as the exalted Lord. Truly one of the most remarkable examples of God taking the worst possible situation and turning it into good.

Second, they probably knew the Old Testament story of Joseph. How his own brothers sold him to slave traders headed to Egypt. How he spent the next seventeen years of his life as a slave, then a prisoner, with no hope of ever getting out. But in an unheard of turn of events, he became lord over all Egypt, second only to Pharaoh.

Years later, when Joseph's brothers came trembling before him, pleading for forgiveness, Joseph said, "Do not fear, for am I in the place of God? [20] As for you, you meant evil against me, but God meant it for good, to bring it about that many people should be kept alive, as they are today" (Genesis 50:19-20).

Joseph's amazing story powerfully demonstrated that God does work all things for good. He can take the worst circumstances, the most disastrous state of affairs, and turn them into something very good. He not only *can* do so, we are promised here that he *will* do so.

It doesn't matter whether our current situation is of our own making, or whether we are the victim of circumstance. In either case, we are promised that all things will eventually work together for our good.

James 1:5

"If any of you lacks wisdom, let him ask God, who gives generously to all without reproach, and it will be given him."

Here at the very beginning of his letter, James promises his readers that anyone who asks God for wisdom will be given it. It applies to everyone, because everyone lacks wisdom to some extent.

And don't miss what James says about God here. That he is a God who gives generously "without reproach." Which means that he gives ungrudgingly. Whether he is giving wisdom or anything else.

I am well aware that in the verses that follow James tells his readers that they must ask for wisdom in faith and without doubt. I will address this in detail in Chapter Three.

Psalm 147:3

"He heals the brokenhearted and binds up their wounds."

This is a little known, but indescribably beautiful promise that tells us (1) that God does care when our hearts are breaking; and (2) he has the power to mend our broken hearts and make them whole again; and (3) he will do it.

So for whatever reason your heart is broken—rejection, betrayal, disappointment, loss, failure, or the crumbling of your dreams—bring this promise in hand to God and ask him to keep this promise for you: To heal your heart and put the pieces of your life back together again. He will.

Psalm 37:4-5

"Delight yourself in the LORD, and he will give you the desires of your heart. 5 Commit your way to the LORD; trust in him, and he will act.

In this psalm David addresses a common tendency. We can easily become envious of those who are prospering when we are not. Especially when those who prosper are "wicked." The first verse of Psalm 37 clearly states the theme: "Do not fret because of evildoers; be not envious of wrongdoers!"

So it is against this background that the promise of verses four and five is presented.

"Delight yourself in the LORD" means, "Enjoy God like you would enjoy the prosperity you want if you had it. Take pleasure in him like you would take pleasure in the possessions you wish you had. Be thankful you have HIM, even though at present, it may seem like you don't have much else compared to others. Enjoy God, smile and be patient. Your time will come."

When we are in the throes of self-pity because we have so little compared to others, it is difficult to delight ourselves in the LORD. Our default attitude is usually something more like "Be bitter and sullen before the LORD because you feel shortchanged and unfairly treated."

When we do delight in him (our delighting doesn't have to be perfectly consistent!), we are promised that he will give us the desires of our hearts.

I love this promise and like to quote it when I hear people say, "God never promised to give us what we want, just what we need." I like to say, "Actually . . . he *has* promised to give us what we want. He's promised to give us the desires of our hearts as a matter of fact!

And, yes, it is true that when we learn to delight in the LORD, even in our deprivation, it will most definitely affect the kinds of desires we have.

A final thought. David is speaking from personal experience. He wrote this psalm when he was king, later in life. But before he got there, he went through many years of poverty and difficulties. Yet through it all we see him (usually) delighting in God in praise and thanksgiving, committing his undertakings to him, trusting him and waiting for him to fulfill the promise he had made to him. In the end, he learned God does act and does give us the desires of our hearts.

Isaiah 49:14-16

> "But Zion said, "The LORD has forsaken me; my Lord has forgotten me." [15] "Can a woman forget her nursing child, that she should have no compassion on the son of her womb? Even these may forget, yet I will not forget you.""

Has it ever seemed that God has forgotten you? That he has forsaken you? Then this promise is for you.

Isaiah 49 is a Messianic prophesy. Through Isaiah, God tells his people that though they currently were suffering as exiles in captivity, the day was coming when his Servant, the Messiah, would redeem them and set them free. The day was coming when their fortunes would be restored.

The people heard God's word spoken through Isaiah. But they struggled to believe it. Because what they felt and what they were experiencing was the opposite; which is why they said, "The LORD has forsaken me; my Lord has forgotten me."

To convince them how unthinkable and impossible it is that he could ever forget them and stop loving them, God sets before them the greatest love human beings have to offer. That of a mother for her young child.

"Can a woman forget her nursing child that she should have no compassion on the child she gave birth to?" The obvious answer to this question is, "Of course not. How could a mother possibly forget this little one suckling at her breast, and not love that baby with all the love she had to offer? She never would or could forget." God says, "Even these may forget. But I will not forget you."

God's love for you is greater than that of a mother for her nursing child. He will never forget or forsake you, no matter what your feelings or circumstances may be suggesting to you. The time will come again when your circumstances make it easy to believe his love for you—when you'll have no doubt that he is thinking of you and delighting in you. Hang on!

Psalm 77:14

"You are the God who works wonders; you have made known your might among the peoples."

What I absolutely love about this implied promise is its context! You really must read all of Psalm 77 to appreciate it fully.

In Psalm 77, the psalmist Asaph is crying out to God for help in his trouble. Yet all he gets in response is silence.

So he asks several heart-wrenching questions. "Has the LORD's steadfast love forever ceased? Are his promises at an end for all time? Has God forgotten to be gracious? Has he in anger shut up his compassion" (Psalm 77:8-9).

So he decides to focus on the miracles that God had done in the past. In doing this he comes to his senses and realizes that the God who did great miracles in the past also does them in the present. His God is a God that did and does work wonders. He is a God that did and still does keep his promises.

His God is our God. He will do wonders in your life.

Matthew 11:28-29

"Come to me, all who labor and are heavy laden, and I will give you rest. [29] Take my yoke upon you, and learn from me, for I am gentle and lowly in heart, and you will find rest for your souls."

Here, Jesus promises rest to people who are suffering from a particular kind of weariness. The weariness that comes from false beliefs. The word translated "rest" is a Greek verb that also can be rendered "revive" or "refresh." So Jesus is promising strength as well as rest.

The people of Jesus' day had been heavily burdened by the teaching of the Pharisees in particular. The Pharisees weren't content with teaching the people what God had commanded as recorded in the Torah. They invented new commandments. They multiplied rules and laws. The real problem is that they told the people that their new commandments must be kept—all of them—if they hoped to please God and be accepted by him.

At another time Jesus said about them, "They tie up heavy burdens, hard to bear, and lay them on people's shoulders, but they themselves are not willing to move them with their finger" (Matthew 23:4).

So this promise especially applies to people who are loaded down with unnecessary commandments they are laboring to keep in order to be accepted by God. And loaded down with guilt because they know they haven't kept them.

To these guilt-ridden souls, Jesus says, "Come to me . . . and I will give you rest." Those who come to Jesus (believe in him as Savior) find rest and strength because those who believe in him no longer have to keep any commandments to be accepted by God. Christ has atoned for their sins on the cross. He has kept the Law for them. They are saved by grace not by works. So they gladly strive to keep God's commandments—not to be saved—but because they have already been saved.

Luke 18:27

"But Jesus said, "What is impossible with men is possible with God.""

We all encounter crises, problems or obstacles that go way beyond our ability to solve or overcome. That defy all attempts to resolve, even when calling upon the accumulated knowledge and experience of the best and brightest. We also face impossibilities imposed by the laws of nature themselves.

In this saying, Jesus reminds us of God's omnipotence. That his power knows no bounds. That though we can't, God can. Whatever is impossible to us—whether it truly is or we only think it is—is not impossible to God. Because there are no impossibilities for God. Because he is Creator of everything, everything in the created realm can be changed and altered by him at will.

So for every one of our unsolvable problems, God not only has one solution, but innumerable solutions.

Though nothing specific is promised in this saying of Jesus, something implied is promised. In fact, the teaching that nothing is impossible to God would be, at best, a curiosity, and at worst, a cruelty, if it wasn't also true that God wants to use this power for our benefit. Which we know to be true because the Bible in so many other places tells us this.

Your God can do anything. Though what you currently face has overwhelmed you with its complexity or hopelessness, he can easily help you and easily solve your problem. And he will do so.

So when you face an impossible situation that overwhelms you, go to him in prayer, and say, "God, it is written that the things that are impossible for us are possible for you. Therefore, I call upon you to do what I can't, and solve this problem, and give me what only you can."

Mark 9:23

"All things are possible for one who believes."

What an awesome promise. Mark 9 records that a distraught father brought his demon-possessed son to Christ's disciples in order that they might heal him. Stricken by the demon since childhood, no one had been able to heal him. Nothing worked. Unfortunately, the disciples couldn't do it either.

When Jesus arrived on the scene, the demon thrashed the boy and he fell to the ground. The distraught father pleaded with Jesus, "If you can do anything, please help us!" Jesus replied in amazement, "'If you can?!' All things are possible for one who believes." The father answered, "I believe. Help my unbelief." Jesus immediately cast out the demon and healed the son.

Did you notice the juxtaposition of this saying of Jesus with the previous one in Luke 18:27? There he said that the things that are impossible for men are possible for God." But here he says, "All things are possible for one who believes." In other words, not only are all things possible for God, but all things are also possible for one who believes all things are possible for God!

In Matthew's version of this same story (17:20), Jesus tells his disciples that if they had faith the size of a mustard seed that nothing would be impossible for them.

Lamentations 3:25

"My soul is bereft of peace; I have forgotten what happiness is; [18] so I say, "Gone is my glory, and all that I had hoped for

from the LORD." ¹⁹ The thought of my affliction and my
homelessness is wormwood and gall! ²⁰ My soul continually
thinks of it and is bowed down within me. ²¹ But this I call to
mind, and therefore I have hope: ²² The steadfast love of the
LORD never ceases, his mercies never come to an end; ²³ they
are new every morning; great is your faithfulness. ²⁴ "The
LORD is my portion," says my soul, "therefore I will hope in
him." ²⁵ The LORD is good to those who wait for him, to the
soul that seeks him" (NRS).

The promises in this passage are perfect for the those who has been
suffering for so long that they have forgotten what it feels like to be
happy. The one who sees and feels nothing but sorrow and darkness.
That is exactly how the prophet Jeremiah, whose words these are, felt.

The book of Lamentations contains the prophecies of Jeremiah after
the complete destruction of Jerusalem by the Babylonians. The book is
literally one long lament from beginning to end.

Practically all the people had been taken away as captives to
Babylon. And, even though Jeremiah knew that the appalling
destruction was coming, nothing could have prepared him for the
actual horrifying event and its tragic aftermath.

He walked the deserted streets witnessing the carnage all around
him. Everything was destroyed. The temple had been razed to the
ground. Its priests had been murdered within. Dead bodies lay
everywhere. The few people left were starving for lack of food. He
heard children crying to their mothers for something to eat.

Then in chapter 3, Jeremiah gives vent to his sorrow and bitterness.
In stark honesty he reveals his feelings of torment to all. The verses
above are a part of that.

But then, remarkably, Jeremiah's spirit brightens. He does
something important. He stops looking and thinking about the bad in
front of him; he starts thinking instead about something else. He
remembers something that gives him hope. Four related things. He
starts conversing with himself.

"But this I call to mind, and therefore I have hope:

(1) "The steadfast love of the LORD never ceases, his mercies never
come to an end; they are new every morning."

Jeremiah reminds himself who God really is. That he is a God of
steadfast love. He loves us with a love that never lets us go. That he
never stops being merciful. That his mercies are new every morning.
That though today may be a day of devastation and sorrow, and it may

seem and feel like it will never change, God will be merciful again.

(2) "Great is your faithfulness."

He reminds himself that God's faithfulness is great. Even when we are faithless, and turn from him, he remains faithful to us. He remains faithful to his promises, and will still keep them for us.

(3) "The LORD is my portion, says my soul. Therefore I have hope in him."

He reminds himself that though he has no "portion" (possessions/property/inheritance) left, the LORD, his God is his portion. Because God is powerful, merciful and faithful, that gives Jeremiah hope. There is nothing else that gives Jeremiah hope. Certainly nothing that he sees or hears gives him hope. But because he has God, he has hope.

(4) "The LORD is good to those who wait for him, to the soul who seeks him."

He reminds himself what all the saints of old knew and experienced. That those who continue to wait for God to keep his promises, discover that eventually he does. Always. Those who refuse to give up on God will experience his goodness again, no matter how hopeless life may now seem.

Ephesians 3:20-21

"Now to him who is able to do immeasurably more than all we ask or imagine, according to his power that is at work within us, [21] to him be glory in the church and in Christ Jesus throughout all generations, for ever and ever! Amen" (NIV).

These words are what is known as a *doxology*. From a Greek word that means "to glorify" or "to praise," a doxology is a short hymn of praise to God. It may have been part of an ancient hymn or liturgy that Paul chose to quote.

Paul ascribes to God an awesome ability. He is the one who has the power to do immeasurably more than all we could ever ask or imagine.

What's so awesome about this ability? Just this: God is not limited by our prayers, thinking or dreams. He can, and wants to, give us infinitely beyond whatever we can think to ask him. He has the power and the desire to do for us infinitely more than whatever we can imagine or dream.

My experience has been that most people are very conservative in what they ask God. They don't ask him for much. Because they don't want to be greedy or selfish, perhaps. This passage reminds us that God is far more willing and able to give than we are to ask.

Moreover, we all find ourselves in situations in which we can't think what to ask or what to do. Maybe what we face is just too complicated. So what we end up asking can be shortsighted, misguided, or just not enough. Or we just run out of ideas.

This passage reminds us that God has us covered. He doesn't limit himself to the letter of our request. Nor is he limited by our ideas. He is willing and able to give immeasurably more than what we can think to ask or think to do.

CHAPTER THREE – BELIEVING GOD'S PROMISES

Promises and faith go together. God's promises are what Christian faith believes. Faith is the way we benefit from God's promises.

In fact, most of God's promises only benefit us if we believe them.

For example, consider Christ's promise of prayer, "Ask, and it will be given you" (Matthew 7:7). Only those who believe the promise to be true—that God will actually keep it—will bother to ask. Only those who ask will benefit from this promise.

Jesus was speaking of the important relationship between faith and promises when he said to Martha in John 11, "I am the resurrection and the life. Whoever believes in me, though he die, yet shall he live . . . Do you believe this?" He was inquiring whether she believed because he knew that only then would she benefit from the promise.

Fortunately for her, Martha did believe the promise: "She said to him, 'Yes, Lord; I believe that you are the Christ, the Son of God, who is coming into the world'" (John 11:25-27).

Faith plays the same crucial role in human promises.

Let's say you had a wealthy grandfather who promised you in a letter that he had set up a bank account for you and deposited 10 million dollars in it for your use. If you didn't consider your grandfather trustworthy, you wouldn't believe his promise. If you didn't believe his promise you wouldn't bother to drive to the bank to check it out. Which would mean you would never benefit from the money in any way—even though the huge sum that he set aside for you was there all the time.

So whether we're dealing with divine or human promises, most of them will only benefit you if you believe them.

Not Much Impressed Jesus . . . But This Did

When we read the four Gospels it is pretty clear that very little impressed Jesus. In fact, I can only think of several times that something did. It is striking that in two of those cases it was someone's faith that impressed him.

The Centurion's Faith

The first person whose faith impressed him was a centurion, a Roman imperial officer who had command over one hundred soldiers. Matthew records the incident in chapter eight of his gospel.

> "When Jesus had entered Capernaum, a centurion came to him, asking for help. [6] "Lord," he said, "my servant lies at home paralyzed and in terrible suffering." [7] Jesus said to him, "I will go and heal him." [8] The centurion replied, "Lord, I do not deserve to have you come under my roof. But just say the word, and my servant will be healed. [9] For I myself am a man under authority, with soldiers under me. I tell this one, 'Go,' and he goes; and that one, 'Come,' and he comes. I say to my servant, 'Do this,' and he does it." [10] When Jesus heard this, he was astonished and said to those following him, "I tell you the truth, I have not found anyone in Israel with such great faith . . . Then Jesus said to the centurion, "Go! It will be done just as you believed it would." And his servant was healed at that very hour." (Matthew 8:5-10,13 NIV).

Jesus was astonished by the centurion's faith, claiming that it was a faith he had never seen in anyone before. What was it about the centurion's faith that impressed Jesus so?

I think it was the matter-of-fact way the centurion compared his position of authority over those who served him to Jesus' position of authority over his servant's paralysis. In the mind of the centurion, it was simply a matter of authority.

Just as a soldier must give immediate and unquestioning obedience to a superior officer, so his servant's sickness had to give immediate and unquestioning obedience to Jesus, a superior authority. It was as simple as that.

What impressed and amazed Jesus was that the centurion had such clarity about this. Especially since his own disciples were so slow in understanding and believing it.

The Canaanite Woman's Faith

The second person whose faith wowed Jesus was also a Gentile—a woman from the region of Tyre and Sidon. This "Canaanite woman" came to Jesus because of a case of demonic possession. Her daughter was being severely tormented by a demon.

> "And behold, a Canaanite woman from that region came out and was crying, "Have mercy on me, O Lord, Son of David; my daughter is severely oppressed by a demon." [23] But he did not answer her a word. And his disciples came and begged him, saying, "Send her away, for she is crying out after us." [24] He answered, "I was sent only to the lost sheep of the house of Israel." [25] But she came and knelt before him, saying, "Lord, help me." [26] And he answered, "It is not right to take the children's bread and throw it to the dogs." [27] She said, "Yes, Lord, yet even the dogs eat the crumbs that fall from their masters' table." [28] Then Jesus answered her, "O woman, great is your faith! Be it done for you as you desire." And her daughter was healed instantly" (Matthew 15:22-28).

Jesus was so impressed by this woman's faith that he gave her high praise: "O woman, great is your faith!"

So what was it about the Canaanite woman's faith that so wowed Jesus that he called it, "great"? It was that she refused to accept no for an answer.

Nothing that happened to her deterred her from asking until she got what she wanted. And it was that "refuse-to-accept-no-for-an-answer" attitude that Jesus called "great faith." And he gave her what she wanted.

Why didn't she give up? Because she was unswervingly convinced that Jesus would help her—despite all appearances to the contrary. Like someone who knows that the sun is shining behind the storm clouds, she intuited his loving heart behind his cold words and demeanor. In a way, she called Jesus' bluff.

Faith Impressed Jesus Like Nothing Else

As you can see, faith impressed and amazed Jesus. By comparison, other than the widow who gave all she had (Mark 12:41-44), I can't think of a case in the New Testament in which something other than faith amazed Jesus. Not love or holiness. Not zeal or humility. Not any of the things that impress and amaze most people. Like success, winning, intelligence, power, talent, authority, strength, confidence, or beauty. Or status symbols like wealth, possessions and accomplishments. None of that seemed to impress Jesus whatsoever.

Actually, you would think nothing would cause the Son of God incarnate to marvel. All things were made through him. If anyone had seen it all, he had seen it all. Nevertheless, seeing someone display a faith that believed that he both could (he was all-powerful) and would (he was gracious and faithful) help them caused him to marvel.

Why did that kind of faith impress Jesus? Because it was rare? Yes!

Faith and Doubt

Not everyone has faith as extraordinary as the centurion or the woman of Canaan. Nor do they need to.

To benefit from God's promises we just have to believe them.

But what does that mean? What is this faith that believes God's promises? In this section we'll take a closer look at what faith is, and isn't.

What is the Point?

But before we do, I want to make as clear as I possibly can the real point I'm making in this chapter. So I need to return to something I complained about in the Introduction.

I'm concerned that many Christians have been seduced. As a result they no longer really expect what God has promised to happen, if they ever did. Instead they read God's promises to feel better. That's really all they expect. It's really all they want. So if reading one of God's promises makes their worry go away, for example, they're more than satisfied.

But they don't really expect what God promised to happen. Which is the whole point of God's promises.

Either because of errant teaching, disappointing experience, or both, when they ask God something in prayer, they are never sure that God will give them what they ask. Instead, their default attitude is, "I hope God gives me what I asked. We'll just have to wait and see." That isn't faith. It's doubt.

The whole idea that they are supposed to be sure that God will give them what they asked—which is what faith is—is foreign to them.

They are completely missing the point of God's promises and what it means to believe them. So keep this section in mind as you read through the rest of the chapter. If I seem especially critical of doubt, that's why.

Faith Defined

When we seek to define faith, the obvious "go to" passage would appear to be Hebrews 11:1: "Now faith is the assurance of things hoped for, and the conviction of things not seen." Unfortunately, the Greek word translated "assurance" (*hypostasis*) is nowhere else used in that way. Neither in the Bible nor in any other extant ancient Greek text in our possession. It typically means "substance," as it does in Hebrews 11:3. So to translate it as "assurance" is probably wrong.

The second half of the verse, on the other hand, does contain part of the definition of faith. It is the conviction of things not seen. Faith is believing that something is true or real, even though we can't see it; even though there is no empirical evidence.

A better "proof passage" for faith is Romans 4:20-21, in which Paul is discussing Abraham's faith.

> "No distrust made him waver [doubt] concerning the promise of God, but he grew strong in his faith as he gave glory to God, [21] fully convinced that God was able to do what he had promised."

A little background. In chapter four of his letter to the Romans, Paul is discussing what is meant by the pivotal Genesis passage, "And Abraham believed God, and it was reckoned to him as righteousness" (Genesis 15:6). Specifically he is attempting to prove that Abraham was saved/justified by faith and not by the works of the Law of Moses. In this connection he defines what the faith was that Abraham had.

What Abraham believed in Genesis 15 was God's promise to him that he would have a multitude of descendants. Actually, it's better than that. What Abraham believed was a promise that God had first made to him several years before, but still hadn't kept.

> "After these things the word of the LORD came to Abram in a vision: "Fear not, Abram, I am your shield; your reward shall be very great." [2] But Abram said, "O Lord GOD, what will you give me, for I continue childless, and the heir of my house is Eliezer of Damascus?" [3] And Abram said, "Behold, you have given me no offspring, and a member of my household will be my heir." [4] And behold, the word of the LORD came to him: "This man shall not be your heir; your very own son shall be your heir." [5] And he brought him outside and said, "Look toward heaven, and number the stars, if you are able to number them." Then he said to him, "So shall your offspring

be." [6] And he believed the LORD, and he counted it to him as righteousness"(Genesis 15:1-6).

God had already promised Abraham at least three times that he would give him a multitude of descendants. That a great nation would come from him. That his descendants would be more than the stars of heaven and the sand on the shore.

So when God appeared to Abraham again and told him his reward would be very great, he wasn't thrilled. He sounds a little disgruntled, in fact. Even surly. "God you keep promising me that I will have a multitude of descendants, but I'm still childless! You have given me no offspring! I'm already an old man! I hear your promise. But you still haven't given me what you promised."

God didn't fulfill his promise then and there. He didn't give Abraham some kind of indisputable proof. He simply repeated the promise for the fourth or fifth time.

I can almost hear Abraham audibly sighing just before he said, "I believe you. Even though I still have no child. Even though it has been years since you first promised it and I still have nothing. Despite all that, I believe you, God. I believe that you will do for me what you have promised. I believe that you will fulfill your promise to me."

To me, knowing what came before makes Abraham's faith more meaningful. Anyone can believe a promise when it is first made. But to continue to believe it when years have passed and all you have are the words—that is faith. That is the faith that Abraham reaffirmed in Genesis 15. That is the faith he expressed. That is the faith that God reckoned to him as righteousness.

That is the faith that Paul is describing in Romans 4 as the crux of his teaching that we all are justified by faith. It is faith that believes that God will do what he has promised, even after years have passed, and the thing promised is still only a promise.

> "No distrust made him waver concerning the promise of God, but he grew strong in his faith as he gave glory to God, [21] fully convinced that God was able to do what he had promised. [22] That is why his faith was "counted to him as righteousness.""

That faith, Paul points out, is the opposite of doubt or wavering. It is being "fully convinced" that God is able to do what he has promised.

But it is also what Paul doesn't say. This faith is also being fully convinced that God WILL DO what he has promised.

The Greek word that is translated "fully convinced" is *plērophoria*, which, according to the authoritative BDAG Greek lexicon, means a "state of complete certainty, full assurance, certainty."

Not just "certainty" . . . but a "state of complete certainty"!

Perfect.

Abraham had every reason to doubt God's promise. But he fought through the doubt and continued to believe that God would do for him what he had promised to do. He continued to be certain that God would do what he had promised.

That is what faith is. That is what faith does.

A Definition of Faith

So here it is. Faith is being certain that God will keep his promises. **Faith is certain that whatever God has promised will happen. No matter how long it takes. No matter what happens in the meantime.** Faith is certain, confident, sure and fully convinced that God will fulfill his promise.

Doubt Defined

To doubt means to be uncertain about something. To be unsure.

We saw this in the Romans passage quoted above. There to doubt meant to be unsure of whether God is able to keep his promise. "No distrust made Abraham doubt . . . he was fully convinced that God was able to do what he had promised."

There are two key passages in the New Testament that speak of doubt. To get a fuller understanding we'll look at those next.

James 1:5-8

In Chapter 2 we read the beautiful promise of wisdom contained in the first chapter of the letter of James. Now we need to look more closely at the surrounding verses. Because in those verses James addresses the subject of doubt.

> "If any of you lacks wisdom, let him ask God, who gives generously to all without reproach, and it will be given him. [6] But let him ask in faith, with no doubting, for the one who doubts is like a wave of the sea that is driven and tossed by the wind. [7] For that person must not suppose that he will receive anything from the Lord; [8] he is a double-minded man, unstable in all his ways" (James 1:5-8).

James promises his readers that if any among them lacks wisdom, let him ask God, and it will be given him. "But," he writes, "let him ask in faith, with no doubting."

The first thing I want you to notice is that James pits these two against one another as opposites:

"ask in faith"<-- >"doubting."

Let's look specifically at how James describes doubt.

He first compares a doubter to waves battered by the wind: "the one who doubts is like a wave of the sea that is driven and tossed by the wind." James uses this colorful metaphor to communicate what goes on in a doubter's mind.

Just as a wave is blown first one way then another by the wind, so the doubter's conviction of whether God is going to give him what he asked—wisdom, in this case—goes back and forth between being sure that God is going to do it, and being unsure. He wavers back and forth between these two opinions.

Because he does this, the doubter is "a double-minded man." In other words, the doubter is of two minds. One that is certain that God will keep his promise. And one that isn't. The doubter, "is unstable in all his ways." The Greek word translated "unstable" can also mean "restless" and it is sometimes used to refer to a person who vacillates in his convictions.

According to James, the real problem with doubting is that it leads to an unfortunate consequence. The person who asks in doubt "shouldn't think that he will receive anything from the Lord" (1:7).

Pay attention to what James doesn't write. He doesn't write anything about *why* the person is doubting, or *what* they are doubting.

Whether, for example, they are doubting God's power or are doubting his willingness. Whether they are doubting because they're unsure if God *can* give them wisdom, or are doubting because they're unsure if God *will* give them wisdom.

For James, a person who asks in doubt is simply a person who is unsure or unconvinced—for any reason—that what they ask will be given.

Before You Get Discouraged, Read This

At the heart of James's definition of doubt is the notion of wavering. Of going back and forth between believing/being sure that God will give you what you asked and doubting/being unsure that he will. The second point he makes is that a doubter shouldn't expect God to answer their prayer.

It sounds as if he is saying that unless we are doubt-free God won't answer our prayers. That if any doubt whatsoever enters our minds while we are waiting for God to answer our prayer, we guarantee that God will not grant whatever we asked.

While what James says may be true according to the letter of the law, fortunately God is a God of grace and mercy. As you'll see later in the chapter, he is a God that has frequently been merciful to doubters.

The doubt that ruins our prayers is not the fleeting thoughts of uncertainty that all Christians have while they wait. It is allowing uncertainty to gain the upper hand for extensive periods. Or never being sure in the first place, as I said earlier. I'll have more to say about this a little later.

Mark 11:22-24

You should recognize Mark 11:24 from Chapter two. It was one of the promises of prayer featured there. Here, though, I want to focus on the verse before it, 11:23, as it is one of the only places where Jesus addressed the topic of doubt.

> "And Jesus answered them, 'Have faith in God. [23] Truly, I say to you, whoever says to this mountain, 'Be taken up and thrown into the sea,' and does not doubt in his heart, but believes that what he says will come to pass, it will be done for him. [24] Therefore I tell you, whatever you ask in prayer, believe that you have received it, and it will be yours.'"

The day before Jesus spoke the words above, he had cursed a fig tree with the words, "May no one ever eat fruit from you again." So as they passed the fig tree, the disciples noticed that it had withered down to its roots. Amazed, Peter said to Jesus, "Rabbi, look! The fig tree that you cursed has withered." Hearing this, Jesus used the fig tree, and the disciples' amazement, as an opportunity to talk about faith and doubt.

Essentially, he told them, "Why are you amazed? Have faith in God! The fig tree I cursed withered because I had faith in God. What I did you can do too. The fig tree withered because I believed that what I spoke to it would happen. If seeing a fig tree wither impresses you, then consider this. Whoever says to this mountain, 'Be lifted up and be thrown into the sea,' and does not doubt in his heart, but believes that what he says will happen, it will be done for him."

To make it clear what Jesus is saying, let's drop out the phrase "and does not doubt in his heart"

Whoever says to this mountain, 'Be lifted up and be thrown into the sea . . . and believes that what he says will happen, it will be done for him.''

In other words, what will cause the mountain to be thrown into the sea—the deciding factor—is that the person believes that what he says will happen.

Now let's put the doubt phrase back in.

"Whoever says to this mountain, "Be lifted up and be thrown into the sea, **and does not doubt in his heart**, but believes that what he says will happen, it will be done for him.

Clearly, Jesus is saying that doubt has the effect of nullifying the command, "Be lifted up and thrown into the sea," ensuring that it won't happen. But he is also saying that whereas faith is being certain that what you say (or pray) will happen, doubt is not being certain.

Faith is being certain that whatever one says, or prays (11:24), will actually happen. Doubt does not believe it will happen. Or at least isn't sure it will. Faith says, "It will happen." Doubt can't say, "It will happen." At best it can say, "It may happen."

A Definition of Doubt

So on the basis of the foregoing, we're ready for a definition of doubt.

Doubt is being uncertain that what God promised will happen…for whatever reason. Whether the person is doubting because they're unsure that God has *the power* to do what he has promised, on the one hand; or they're doubting because they're uncertain that God has *the willingness*, on the other. Either way it is doubt.

Some people doubt that God will do what he promised because they are unsure that God *can*. Others doubt that he will keep his promises because they are unsure that God *wants to*.

What Makes Us Doubt?

I think that most Christians living at the beginning of the Third Millennium struggle with the kind of doubt that says, "I'm absolutely sure that God *can* give me what he promised. I'm just not sure that he *will*."

And if someone were to ask such a Christian why they're unsure that God will, they might answer in a number of ways. Like this:

"I'm not sure God will give me what I asked:

- "Because I'm not sure it is his will for me. It may not be his will:
    - "because what I'm asking is sinful in his sight," or
    - "because what I'm asking is something that is bad for me—something that will harm me," or
    - "because it is not part of the plan he has laid out for my life," or
    - "because he knows it isn't something I really need, just something I want," or
    - "because it doesn't bring God glory or further his kingdom."

- "Because I'm not sure whether I'm living a sufficient Christian life.
    - "Maybe God thinks that I'm not loving enough, or going to church enough, or reading the Bible enough, or praying enough, or giving enough, or repenting enough, or using my talents enough, or being holy enough, or selfless enough, or humble enough," or
    - "There might be something that I'm doing that is sinful in God's sight that I need to stop doing before he'll keep his promise," or
    - "There might be something that he expects me to do that I have to start doing," or
    - "Maybe I'm not asking with pure motives or for the right reasons. Maybe I'm asking to spend it on my pleasures."

- "Because he just may not want to. God is God, after all. He can do whatever he wants to do for whatever reason."

At the risk of being redundant, let me say it once more. Faith is being certain that what God has promised will happen. Doubt is not being sure it will happen—for whatever reason.

So if whenever you ask God for something, you can't say for sure whether he will give it to you, that is doubt. Even if the reason you can't be sure is that you don't know whether it is God's will or not. It is still doubt.

And because you are doubting, you are making it far less likely God will give you what you ask, as James pointed out in James 1:7.

In the following quote, the reformer Martin Luther beautifully summarizes everything we've learned about faith and doubt in this chapter, but in a far more memorable way!

> So then, before a person begins to pray, he should examine and probe himself to ascertain whether he believes or doubts that his prayer will be fulfilled. If he finds that he doubts or is uncertain, or that he prays at random, the prayer is nothing. His heart is not constant; it wavers and wobbles back and forth, and it is impossible for God to put anything into such a heart, even as you cannot drop anything into a person's hand if he does not hold it still (Martin Luther, "An Explanation of the Lord's Prayer for Simple Layman – 1519," AE 42:76).

Could anyone say it better than that? Luther says two things in this quote. First, before we pray we should examine ourselves to see whether we actually believe that our prayer will be fulfilled. If we aren't certain, if we doubt, our prayer is nothing. God won't give us what we ask.

Second, with an amazing little metaphor Luther suggests to us what doubt must look like to God. Just as it is impossible to drop something into a person's hand if they never hold it still . . . so it is impossible for God to give anything to a doubting heart that wavers and wobbles back and forth.

That is what doubting is. That is what doubting does. That is what doubting looks like to God.

"If It Be Your Will"

If all the reasons for doubting were ranked, I have no "doubt" that number one on the list would be *doubting because of God's will*.

It works like this. As we saw in Chapter 2, Jesus promises that God will give us what we ask. Nevertheless, most Christians can't say for sure that what they have asked God will happen. Why not? Because what they've asked may not be God's will.

But if doubting means being uncertain that what you've asked God will happen . . . and you can't ever be sure that what you've asked will happen, because it may not be God's will . . . then you are constantly doubting when you pray.

So it makes me wonder whether we should even think about whether something we're asking God is his will or not. Otherwise we will almost always be doubting. With the consequence that God won't give us what we ask.

But didn't Jesus teach us to pray, "Thy will be done on earth as it is in heaven?" He did. But it is my belief that this is simply another way of saying, "Father in heaven, everything that happens in heaven happens according to your will. Let the same be true on earth. Let not the will of kings and potentates, legislatures and judges, or any human authority control human events. Let your will control all events on earth, like it does in heaven." Interestingly, in Luke's version of the Lord's Prayer the "Thy will be done" petition isn't even there (Luke 11:2-4).

But isn't that the way Jesus prayed in the Garden of Gethsemane? Didn't he pray, "My Father, if it be possible, let this cup pass from me; nevertheless, not as I will, but as you will" (Matthew 26:39)? Yes, but Jesus' prayer in Gethsemane was not a typical prayer request, to say the least.

This was not a case of Jesus asking something that might or might not be God's will. This was a case where God's will was crystal clear. Jesus had to be crucified. It was the reason he came into the world. He was asking if it was possible to get out of it. He was asking the very opposite of the express will of God.

So the fact that he said, "Your will be done," was his way of telling his Father that he was ready to submit to God's will, even though everything inside him was recoiling in terror at that will.

So to see his, "Not my will but yours be done" as a paradigm for every prayerful request is misguided. I would venture to say that the typical Christian doesn't ask God for many things that they know to be the opposite of God's will—as Jesus did in Gethsemane.

Along the same lines, it has long been customary for some Christians to qualify every prayer request with the words, "If it be your will." Praying, "If it be your will" sounds good. Sounds godly, even.

But, unfortunately, it is just an expression of abject doubt clothed in pious-sounding language. It is nothing more than saying "I have no idea whether what I've asked is actually going to be given or happen," which is nothing more than doubt. Doubt wrapped up in false humility. False humility that says, "Oh God, how can I, an infinitesimally tiny creature, a wretched little sinner, possibly know whether what I'm asking is your will?"

The notion that Christians can't ever know whether something they ask God is his will or not is not a Biblical teaching. In the fifth chapter of his first epistle the apostle John writes, "And this is the confidence that we have toward him, that if we ask anything according to his will he hears us. And if we know that he hears us in whatever we ask, we know that we have the requests that we have asked of him" (1 John 5:14-15).

Please take note. John assumes that it is very possible to know what God's will is. Otherwise his words make no sense. How in the world could we ever, as John wrote, know that God hears us and will give us what we ask, if we can never know whether what we asked is his will?

John's point is that when we ask something of God that we know to be his will we can be absolutely confident that "we have the requests we have asked of him."

Of Course What We Ask May Not Be God's Will . . .

Of course what we ask may not be God's will! Of course we sometimes ask for things that aren't good for us or another person we're praying for. Of course God sometimes says, "No." Who doesn't know that?

But my point is that if whenever we ask God for something, we aren't sure whether he will give it because it may not be his will, then we are doubting. And someone who prays with doubt will not receive what he is asking.

The fact is, whenever we are uncertain about the outcome because of the "But-it-might-not-be-God's-will" factor, it is doubt.

Whether It is God's Will or Not Doesn't Matter

Ultimately, it doesn't matter if it is God's will. It doesn't matter if he wants to. Whatever God has promised, he must do, whether he "wants to" or not.

That statement is intentionally provocative. The point is that we get so hung up on whether what we're asking is God's will that we forget that **whatever God has promised *is his will*.**

So when Jesus says, for example, "Whatever you ask the Father in my name, he will give it to you (John 16:23)," *that* is God's will. That's what God wants. So we should focus on *that* will, which he has clearly revealed, rather than on his unrevealed will, whether what we're asking is "his will."

The point is that whatever God has promised he MUST do, because he has attached his sacred name and reputation to it. And it is impossible for him to break his promise.

Yes, It is Doubt

I've spent so much time on the "God's will" question because, as I said, I'm convinced it is the number one reason that people doubt God's promises.

But whatever it is that makes you unsure that what God has promised is going to happen is doubt.

So is it doubt when we ask God for something but are uncertain he will give it because it may not be something we need, just something we want? Yes, it is doubt.

Is it doubt when we are unsure that God will give us what we ask because we've been asking him for the same thing for a long time and haven't received it, and we think, "If he was going to give it he would have done it by now"? Yes, it is doubt.

Is it doubt when we are uncertain that God will give us what we ask because we think of times that God didn't give us what we asked in the past and think, "It's not going to happen. He didn't give it then. He probably won't give it now"? Yes, it is doubt.

Whatever it is that makes us unsure that what God has promised will happen is doubt.

"You're Wasting Your Time"

God: "What are you doing?"
Christian: "I'm praying. I'm asking you for something."
God: No, you're not. You may think you're praying. But you're not. Actually, you're wasting your time."

This is a little conversation I imagine God having with someone who asks for something but isn't sure that God will actually give it.

To the one who asks him for something but isn't sure that he will give it, God says, "You're wasting your time. If and when you decide that you really want to pray, then make your request. When you are certain that I will give you what you ask, then pray to me.

"But this business of asking me for something and then saying, 'I hope God gives it to me. Time will tell,' is nothing but doubt. When you pray that way you're wasting your time and trying my patience. Only the one who asks in faith will get anything from me."

Praying Without Doubt

Let me make this as clear as I can. Everyone doubts after they've asked God for something and are waiting for it to be given. To some extent. Especially if they've been waiting a long time. But God doesn't expect us to have perfect certainty. He doesn't disqualify our prayers if he sees an element of doubt.

What God expects is that we fight the doubt. That we talk back to it.

That we don't let it take up permanent residence in our minds.

I am now convinced that whenever we ask God anything and are waiting for it to be given, the wisest practice is to strive to put out of our mind any thought that makes us unsure that God will grant it.

Like the thought that what we're asking may not be God's will, for example. Or that it may not be something that we really need. Or that our Christian life may not be good enough. Or that we asked for similar things in the past and God didn't give them. Or whatever it might be.

Instead we should always assume that whatever we are asking is God's will and is going to happen. Otherwise we will always be doubting.

Faith Fights Doubt

Not that doing that is easy. It is anything but. Especially when we find ourselves facing some great need, it takes effort to "talk back" to the doubts that have decided to have their family reunion in our brains. To talk back to doubt and say, "I don't care what you say, I believe it is impossible for God not to keep his promises. What he has promised to me will happen" is not easy.

As Luther puts it, faith is a difficult thing.

> But when God makes a promise of some kind, faith wrestles much and long; for reason, or flesh and blood, regards God's promise as altogether impossible. Therefore faith must wrestle with doubt and against reason. Therefore, faith is an active, difficult and powerful thing" (Martin Luther, "Lectures on Genesis, Chapters 6-14" AE 2:266).

It is not possible for any of us to be doubt-free. Nor do we need to be. What matters is whether we surrender to the doubts or fight through them—talking back to them and reaffirming our belief that God will do what he has promised.

Have Mercy on the Doubter

Near the end of the Book of Jude, he writes, "And have mercy on those who doubt." I'm speculating here, but I think Jude urged Christians to have mercy on those who doubt, because there are clear examples of God doing that very thing. Here are three of them.

Lot Hesitated (Genesis 19)

God sent angels to Sodom to warn Lot and his family to flee the city before he destroyed it. When the day of destruction dawned, Lot still hadn't left. So the angels again urged him, saying, "Up! Take your wife and your two daughters who are here, lest you be swept away in the punishment of the city" (Genesis 19:15).

What did Lot do when he heard this urgent warning? He hesitated! Which is exactly what doubt does. The key Biblical words for doubt can be translated "to hesitate." Doubt hesitates because it is not sure. In this case, apparently Lot wasn't sure if what the angels predicted was actually going to happen.

So what did the angels do? They "seized him and his wife and his two daughters by the hand, the LORD being merciful to him, and they brought him out and set him outside the city" (Genesis 19:16).

The angels did what they did because the God was being merciful to Lot. God had mercy on Lot, the doubter, and saved him despite his doubt.

The Doubting Father (Mark 9)

There is a moving account in the New Testament (I briefly mentioned it in Chapter 2) that illustrates how God shows mercy to someone who is doubting. It also is a clear example of how faith fights through doubt.

A father brought his demon-possessed son to Jesus to have him cast it out. His disciples tried but were unable.

The father told Jesus that his son had been possessed since he was a young child, and then pleaded, "But if you can do anything, please have compassion on us and help us!" Jesus replied, "'If you can!' All things are possible for one who believes." The anguished father cried out, "I believe! Help my unbelief" (Mark 9:22-24).

The father's request, "But if you can do anything, please have compassion on us, and help us," was tinged with doubt. And Jesus called him on it. The father was then completely honest with Jesus. He admitted that both faith and doubt were going on inside of him, though he was ashamed of the doubt. So he asked Jesus to "help" his unbelief. It was his way of telling Jesus that he was fighting the doubt but needed his help.

So what did Jesus do? He showed mercy on this doubting father and cast the demon out of his son. Jesus did this even though the father both believed and doubted.

Peter Sank (Matthew 14)

One of the better known miracles of Jesus is that he walked on water. He had been teaching a large crowd on the eastern side of the

Sea of Galilee, but he wasn't finished. So he told his disciples to leave without him and that he would catch up later. So they set sail and began the journey to the other side.

Hours later, the disciples hadn't yet reached the shores of Galilee. It was extremely windy and the waves were turbulent. In the fourth watch of the night (3:00 to 6:00 am) they looked up and saw someone walking on the water and nearing the boat. But they couldn't tell who it was.

Jesus told them it was he and not to be afraid. Peter still wasn't sure and called out, "Lord if it is you, command me to come to you on the water." Jesus said, "Come!"

Peter had such confidence in this word of Jesus, that he stepped out of the boat and began walking on the water toward Jesus. But Peter's faith didn't last. "But when he saw the wind, he was afraid, and beginning to sink, he cried out, 'Lord, save me!'"

What did Jesus do? He had mercy on doubting Peter. "Jesus immediately reached out his hand and took hold of him, saying to him, 'O you of little faith, why did you doubt?'" (Matthew 14:30-31). Jesus was not happy about Peter's doubt. He mildly rebuked him. But despite the doubt, he had mercy on Peter and kept him from sinking.

Faith Affirmations

One of the ways I talk back to doubts is by using faith affirmations. These are either statements or short prayers that affirm my faith in God's promises in the face of doubt. Such as:

- Saying, "Amen! What God has promised me will surely happen" (see the next section).
- Thanking God exactly as I would if he had already fulfilled his promise. Thanking him as if whatever he has promised has already happened (remember Mark 11:24?).
- Saying, "It's just a matter of time. It's not a matter of "if" what God has promised will happen, but "when" it will happen.
- Saying, "I have no doubt that what I have asked will happen. I have no doubt that God will give me what I've asked."
- Saying, "I can't wait!" just as you would about some future event that is certain.
- Saying, "God promised to give me whatever I ask. End of discussion."

- Praying, "I don't know why it is taking so long, Father. I don't need to know. But I know that it doesn't mean that you've said no. How can I know that? Because you have promised to give us what we ask. You are God. It is impossible for you to break your promise. So either you will give me what I've asked or something better."

The Word "Amen."

Concluding a prayer with the word "Amen," (from the Hebrew אָמֵן and the Greek ἀμήν) is an extremely common practice. It is also an ancient practice dating back to the time of Moses (It is prominently featured in Deuteronomy 27, for example). Far more than simply being a word that indicates that the prayer is over, "amen" is actually a statement of faith.

The word indicates a strong affirmation of whatever has just been stated. It is a strong affirmation that what has been said, or is what is about to be said, is absolutely true or certain. It also can be an expression of faith that means, "let it be so," or "it shall surely be."

It is with this in mind that Martin Luther talks about how the word "amen" expresses the faith we should have whenever we pray.

> The little word "Amen" is of Hebrew or Jewish origin.☐ In German it means that something is most certainly true. It is good to remember that this word expresses the faith that we should have in praying every petition. Christ says, "Whatever you ask in prayer, you will receive, if you have faith." . . . If we conclude our prayer with the word "Amen," spoken with confidence and strong faith, it is surely sealed and heard. But without this conclusion neither the beginning nor the middle of the prayer serves any purpose.

> Therefore the little word "Amen" means the same as truly, verily, certainly. It is a word uttered by the firm faith of the heart. It is as though you were to say, "O my God and Father, I have no doubt that you will grant the things for which I petitioned, not because of my prayer, but because of your command to me to request them and because of your promise to hear me. I am convinced, O God, that you are truthful, that you cannot lie. It is not the worthiness of my prayer, but the certainty of your truthfulness, that leads me to believe this firmly. I have no doubt that my petition will become and be

an Amen. (Martin Luther, "An Explanation of the Lord's Prayer for Simple Layman – 1519," AE 42:76)

Understood in this way, the word "amen" is a beautiful statement of faith that says, "What I have just asked, shall surely happen, because God has promised." Or "What God has promised most certainly will happen."

Trustworthy and Truthful

When we trust God, believing that he will do what he says, we are giving him high praise. Because by so doing we show God that we believe he is trustworthy and truthful, which honors him greatly.

Even in human affairs few things we do honor a person more than regarding them as truthful and trustworthy. On the other hand, few things dishonor a person more than saying about him, "Oh, you can't trust anything he says. What he says and what he does are two different things."

For leaders, especially, being considered truthful and trustworthy is everything. Whether they be elected officials or executives in the private sector, their career takes a direct hit when their word can't be trusted. A hit that can be vocationally fatal.

So when you are certain that God will do what he has promised, you glorify him, because you are telling him that you consider him to be what he is: truthful and trustworthy. But when you aren't certain, you call those qualities into question, suggesting that God is unreliable or deceptive.

If you Have No Doubt You'll Be in Heaven When You Die...

The most important of all God's promises is what Jesus and the Apostles called the *gospel*. The good news that when we die we will go to heaven because by his death Christ has atoned for all our sins. Because of what Christ has done, God gives salvation and eternal life freely to all who believe this.

Most Christians I talk to have no doubt that they are going to heaven when they die. Because they believe the gospel promise. They are right to be so certain.

It's pretty obvious that the apostles wanted the recipients of their letters to be certain about where they would be spending eternity.

For example, John writes in his first letter, "I write these things to you who believe in the name of the Son of God that you may know that you have eternal life" (1 John 5:13). Peter tells his readers that they have been born again "to an inheritance that is imperishable, undefiled, and unfading, kept in heaven for you" (1 Peter 1:4).

So given that Christians are certain that God will keep the promise of heaven, I find it strange that many of the same Christians are not certain that God will keep his lesser promises. The promises of prayer, provision, rescue, and the like.

But God's promises are God's promises. If he can be trusted to keep the greatest of his promises, then he can be trusted to keep all his promises. The one making the promise of eternal life is the same one making the other promises. The persons to whom he is making the promises are the same. There is no difference.

Conclusion

But when the Son of Man comes will he find faith on the earth? (Luke 18:8)

Faith is the joyful certainty that God will keep his promises to you. No matter how long it takes. No matter what happens in the meantime.

This faith *expects* God to keep his promises. It doesn't merely hope that he will, or wish that he will. It doesn't ask God for something and then say "maybe." It doesn't assume that whatever has been asked is "probably not God's will." It expects God to give what is requested. It is certain he will do so. And, in humility, it insists that he do so.

Faith is not merely certain that God *can*. It is certain that God *will*.

It wrestles with God. It tells him that an important mark of his deity is his faithfulness in keeping his promises—that he always does what he says he will do. He never lies. He doesn't deceive. His promises contain no fine print.

His promises are not human promises. Lying or failing to keep promises are what created beings do, because of sin or weakness or changing circumstances over which they have no control. But God controls all circumstances. Nothing spins out of his control. He is a Being of limitless power, and everything he has made must do his bidding.

He never changes his mind for *evil*, though he does sometimes allow his mind to be changed for good, when believers storm heaven with their request, and refuse to accept no for an answer. But God never promises something only to later change his mind and refuse to do it.

Faith "reminds" God of all this. It tells God that his reputation is on the line. For he has attached his good name to his promises.

Faith knows that our worthiness or unworthiness has nothing to do with God keeping his promises. He made his promises by grace and he keeps them by grace. Their fulfillment depends on God's character, not ours. Never ours.

This faith is Christian faith. It is the faith by which we are saved. It is the faith the Bible extols from beginning to end. Biblically speaking, it is the only faith there is.

This faith is certain that God will keep every promise he has made. From the greatest to the least. This faith hangs on until the very end. It refuses to give up until what God has promised is given.

And this faith, which believes that God will always keep his promises to you, is one of the most difficult things Christians are called upon to do. This faith is just plain hard.

It is hard because it requires perseverance and patience when the fulfillment of the promise is delayed. It is hard because until the fulfillment comes, it will have to wrestle with *savage* doubts that seek to undermine it.

Hence Jesus' rhetorical question, "When the Son of Man comes will he find faith on the earth?"

By the way, this question comes at the end of a major parable on prayer, the Parable of the Widow and the Unjust Judge. It is as if Jesus is saying, "Will this faith, the faith that is certain that God will give me what I am asking, the faith that refuses to give up, but keeps on asking, and expects God to do what he says he will do, will I find this faith when I come back?"

The purpose of this book is that you might have this faith in God's promises. That you might be inspired and encouraged to believe that it is impossible for God to fail to keep even one of promises. That you might always insist that God be God—the faithful and truthful God who must keep his promises to you and to all Christians. That you might experience God as never before as you experience his faithfulness in keeping his promises to you.

May this book accomplish that purpose in you!

PART II: HOW GOD KEEPS HIS PROMISES

In Part II I am going to show that it is crucial that we understand something about the way God goes about keeping his promises. Because if we don't understand it, we will almost certainly see far fewer promises fulfilled; and our Christian faith itself may be seriously undermined.

God's method of promise keeping is usually not at all what we expected. The good news is that God does have a consistent method when it comes to how he keeps his promises.

A Disclaimer

That said, allow me to put forth the following disclaimer: I will not explain the way God works in your life to your complete satisfaction.

If God is the God we believe him to be—eternal, omnipotent, omniscient, infinite, omnipresent, and creator *ex nihilo,* the God who exists both inside and outside of time, the God who can hear a billion simultaneous prayers and give his full attention to each one—then can anything be more naïve than to assume that we should be able to understand and explain to our satisfaction everything he is doing?

Yet isn't that precisely what many do think? That God should always make sense to them?

So whenever God and his behavior can't be explained to their satisfaction, they doubt him. Whenever God transgresses the boundaries of their intellect, contradicts their moral sensibilities, or just doesn't behave the way they expect, they become bitter or disillusioned. Or they conclude that he doesn't exist; and if he does, he isn't worthy of their time or trust or worship.

But if God is *God,* then isn't it ludicrous to think he must always make sense to us? Isn't it ridiculous to expect him to think as we think, and act as we act in an entirely predictable way?

Now don't misunderstand. Don't think for a moment that I'm suggesting that God never makes sense or never is predictable.

God always keeps his promises. God always does what he says he will do. In this he is perfectly predictable. That is why we can trust him completely. God always is and will be who he has revealed himself to be in the Scriptures: loving, forgiving, faithful, truthful, merciful, powerful, just, wise, good, and gracious. In these things God will always be completely predictable. We can be sure of it.

But the way he chooses to work in our lives is not perfectly predictable.

How and when he goes about his work—which includes the way he fulfills his promises and answers our prayers—can't be predicted with precision. Simply because he is God.

Remember that when God decides how to work in our lives, he takes it *all* in. Unlike us, he sees all ends, all outcomes and all possibilities. He sees all reactions to all actions. He is the God who has counted every conceivable variable and knows them all by name. The God who at once sees how everything affects everything else according to every possible combination.

He is the God who—as he is working in our one life—is simultaneously working in all lives. The God who will always be faithful to his promises, but who also has his own divine agenda. The God who—and the only one who—has *impeccable* timing. The only one who knows when you and everything else is ready.

Are you starting to get it? We are myopic. God is hyperopic. We are shortsighted. God is farsighted. We see the small picture. God sees the big picture. We see what we believe and what we want to see. God sees whatever actually is.

We congratulate ourselves when we think outside the box because our thinking is usually inside the box. God's thinking has no boxes.

We try to plan for all eventualities, which, of course, we can't possibly begin to know. God does know every eventuality. And plans for every single one.

Our minds are finite. God's mind is infinite. What we think is heavily filtered—by our education, our worldview, our culture, our upbringing, our prejudices, our emotions and our experiences, good and bad. God's thinking has no filters.

So why do we cling to the silly assumption that what God is up to in our lives should always make sense to us? Why do we fret when God isn't doing exactly what we thought he would do, or isn't acting exactly when we thought he would? Why do we pout or despair when God is just being himself--a Being who transcends all attempts to limit him?

I'll tell you this, when God said, "As high as the heavens are above the earth, so are my ways above your ways, and my thoughts above your thoughts" (Isaiah 55:8-9), he was being extremely modest. His thoughts and ways are a lot higher above ours than that!

One of the overarching themes of this book is that when you are tempted to doubt or dismiss God because he is working in your life in perplexing or unexpected ways, don't. He never promised to go about his business in ways you would understand. He never promised *that*. But he did promise many glorious things (what this book is about). And what he has promised he will most definitely do. Always.

That God keeps his promises is perfectly predictable. He always will. Of this you can be sure. This you can trust.

How he chooses to work in your life—which includes how he keeps his promises—is usually not what we expected. When we accept that, everything becomes a little easier.

That isn't to say that we can't make *any* sense out of how God keeps his promises. Or that we can't know anything about it. Or that when he goes about fulfilling his promises he acts randomly without any discernible pattern. None of those things are true.

The way God keeps his promises does make some sense. He has in the past followed a fairly consistent pattern. Which, once we understand it, is immensely encouraging and comforting. Which is the whole point of Part II!

God's Role in Suffering

In the following chapters, a particular understanding of God undergirds everything I'm going to write about how God keeps his promises. An understanding that may be a conceptual hurdle for some of you. So I wanted to talk about it here at the beginning of Part II.

I believe that God is all-powerful and all-knowing and that, therefore, nothing can happen unless he permits it. Nothing can happen without his knowledge. The one follows from the other. If things and events can happen that God didn't permit, or know about, then he is no longer all-powerful or all-knowing. If there is someone or something in the universe that can make things happen apart from God's knowledge or power, then he is not all-powerful or all-knowing.

So when something "bad" happens, God had to allow it. He had to know about it. So I would never say about a particular suffering, "God didn't have anything to do with this." God has something to do with everything, both good and bad. God may not have wanted the bad thing to happen. He certainly didn't cause it. God is never the author of evil or pain. But if he hadn't allowed it, it would not have happened.

So what does cause evil and suffering then? In many cases we do. Human beings are the cause of much of the evil in the world. Humankind's lust for wealth, power and fame; their propensity for violence; their intolerance, prejudices and hatred; their shortsightedness that leads them to implement something simply because they know how, before they know if they should. All these sinful qualities and more have brought unfathomable pain and suffering into the world.

On a more personal level, we also bring suffering upon ourselves by our foolish decisions. We decide to do something because it feels right and we end up suffering because of it.

Satan is also a principal author of evil. He deceives and tempts in order to bring about suffering. In both the Old and New Testaments we have evidence that the devil demands—and sometimes receives—permission from God to afflict us (Job 1-2; Luke 22:31-32). In John's Gospel, Christ calls him a murderer (John 8:44). The Apostle Peter calls him, "your enemy . . . who prowls about like a roaring lion seeking someone to devour" (1 Peter 5:8-9; Revelation 2:10).

The rest can be explained by the unfortunate truth that we are living in a fallen world. A world at enmity with God. A world contaminated and infested by rebellion and sin. The fallenness of this world extends to all of nature, resulting in natural disasters or devastating weather. Senseless accidents. Or sickness and disease.

None of this was God's intention when he created this world. The world he made was in harmony with human beings, working with and for them. Not against them. Human beings were created to be authors of good, not agents of suffering and pain. There was to be perfect health and wholeness.

Ultimately all suffering can be viewed as a prelude to death, which violently separates us from each other. But God didn't create death. He intended people to live with him forever. Death was never a part of his perfect blueprint. It was the bitter result of humanity's refusal to obey God and live in harmony with him.

All these things and more cause suffering. But God doesn't cause suffering. Nor does he desire it.

That said, nothing in the universe can happen unless God allows it. Including suffering. It couldn't have happened otherwise.

God's natural tendency is to restrain sinful tendencies in individuals and larger groups of people. He does this because he can see the suffering that will eventually come from it. But if they persist in their evil, and insist on it, he will sometimes step out of the way, and let people go their sinful and painful way. The Apostle Paul makes this point in Romans 1.

What I've written here is, admittedly, highly abbreviated. But it is a key assumption I make throughout the book. You may or may not agree with me, but knowing my theology at the very beginning may ward off confusion later. And even those who disagree with me about God's role in suffering, will still find within the pages to come much that will benefit and help them.

CHAPTER FOUR – GOD'S METHOD OF KEEPING HIS PROMISES: PART I

Introduction

As I hope I've made very clear up to this point, you can count on God to keep his word and do what he says he is going to do. But the way he gets there is frequently anything but a straight line.

As God led the Israelites on a circuitous route to get to the Promised Land, so he seems to do in the fulfilling of all his promises.

So strange does God's promise-keeping method sometimes seem to our thinking that it can be a serious test of faith. We expect him to help us quickly. He leaves us in our trouble. We ask for help. There is only silence. We lay before him our pressing needs and nothing happens.

To any "thinking person" it seems that this loving God is totally ignoring us, has forgotten us, or perhaps even hates and despises us. The silence and the nothingness can be so complete that in our weakest moments we wonder if anyone is even there.

When I say that God makes no sense I'm not merely saying that he contradicts human notions of what is right or proper. It is more than that. I mean that God's way of doing things frequently doesn't even seem to jive with what he has revealed about himself in his written Word, the Bible. I mean he seems to be contradicting himself.

That is why I find the following Bible passages be to be so comforting. Take a moment and read them.

> **Proverbs 3:5** Trust in the LORD with all your heart, and do not lean on your own understanding.

> **Isaiah 55:8-9** For my thoughts are not your thoughts, neither are your ways my ways, declares the LORD. [9] For as the

heavens are higher than the earth, so are my ways higher than your ways and my thoughts than your thoughts.

Those two passages comfort me because they remind me that "what makes sense to me" is a bad way to evaluate what God is doing or has done in my life. As I pointed out at length at the beginning of Part II, our intellect is a flawed unit of measurement when applied to the ways and workings of God.

The two passages remind me that when what God has promised and what makes sense to me clash, I should trust in God's promises and not what makes sense to me.

Martin Luther made this wise observation almost 500 years ago:

> From this one can conclude that although God does not deceive in His promises, He nevertheless reserves their execution for Himself and carries out His promises in such a way that everything seems contradictory and far different from the Word (Martin Luther, "Lectures on Genesis: Chapters 45-50, AE 8:79).

In other words . . . even though God never deceives us with this promises and always keeps them, the way he brings those promises to fulfillment can be so at odds with everything we think we've learned about him in the Bible that it can seem that he has deceived us.

In his commentary on Paul's Letter to the Romans, Luther writes,

> Hence it results that when we pray to God for something, whatever these things may be, and He hears our prayers and begins to give us what we wish, He gives in such a way that He contravenes all of our conceptions.

> . . . For the work of God must be hidden and never understood, even when it happens. But it is never hidden in any other way than under that which appears contrary to our conceptions and ideas (Martin Luther, "Lectures on Romans," AE 25:365).

Translation: The way God goes about answering our prayers and keeping his promises flies in the face of our preconceived notions.

However, just because what is happening in our lives appears to contradict what God promised he would do, doesn't mean that he isn't busy doing it, or won't in time. Just because the answer to your prayer isn't playing out as you thought it would, doesn't mean it isn't playing out.

We would spare ourselves a lot of needless heartache if, when we prayed according to God's promises, we would stop having preconceived ideas of how or when God was going to answer our prayer. God almost never answers our prayers how or when we think he will. We should give up trying to predict the how and the when and the where.

And as we wait, we should take great comfort in what we *can* predict about God. That though he may take us on a long and winding road to get there, in the end God will answer our prayer. God will keep his promises. Of this we can be certain.

That said, I want to stress: There is a method to God's "madness." Though what God is doing often makes no sense to us, there is a divine logic to it. There is a definite pattern that God follows as he goes about fulfilling his promises, repeatedly seen in the pages of the Bible. There is a kind of formula he tends to follow. The remainder of the book will explore this.

God Makes Us Wait

The very first thing to know about how God keeps his promises is that he usually makes us wait . . . a long time. He fulfills his promises far more slowly than we expected. At times, so slowly that it really tests our faith.

Believers of all ages have experienced this.

One of the ways we see this is when the psalmists ask God, "How long?" Or when they cry out, "Make haste (hurry up) to help me!" A few examples will illustrate this.

- How long, O LORD? Will you forget me forever? How long will you hide your face from me? ² How long must I take counsel in my soul and have sorrow in my heart all the day (Psalm 13:1-2)?

- Do not forsake me, O LORD! O my God, be not far from me! ²² Make haste to help me, O Lord, my salvation (Psalm 38:21-22)!

- As for me, I am poor and needy, but the Lord takes thought for me. You are my help and my deliverer; do not delay, O my God (Psalm 40:17)!

- How long, O LORD? Will you hide yourself forever? How long will your wrath burn like fire? ⁴⁷ Remember how short my time is (Psalm 89:46-47)!

- Return, O LORD! How long? Have pity on your servants! [14]
  Satisfy us in the morning with your steadfast love, that we
  may rejoice and be glad all our days (Psalm 90:13-14).

Eventually--and happily--these very same psalmists learned that
waiting for God is most definitely worth it. Because they learned that
he always keeps his promises. So in other places they encourage the rest
of us to wait for God.

- Wait for the LORD; be strong, and let your heart take
  courage; wait for the LORD (Psalm 27:14)!
- Be strong, and let your heart take courage, all you who wait
  for the LORD (Psalm 31:24)!
- Be still before the LORD and wait patiently for him; fret
  not yourself over the one who prospers in his way, over the
  man who carries out evil devices (Psalm 37:7)!
- I waited patiently for the LORD; he inclined to me and
  heard my cry. [2] He drew me up from the pit of destruction,
  out of the miry bog, and set my feet upon a rock, making
  my steps secure (Psalm 40:1-2).

The prophets also take up the same refrain.

- From of old no one has heard or perceived by the ear, no
  eye has seen a God besides you, who acts for those who
  wait for him (Isaiah 64:4).
- The LORD is good to those who wait for him, to the soul
  who seeks him (Lam 3:25).

What does this Waiting Look Like?

So as we're waiting for God to do what he promised, what does this
waiting look like?

First of all, it is the kind of waiting that waits for something that is
definitely going to happen. It is the kind of waiting that eagerly expects
a future event that is certain.

Is there any other kind of waiting? Of course. There is the uncertain
variety. A waiting that doesn't know whether what one is waiting for
will ever happen. Like waiting for the Cubs to win the World Series.
Like waiting to hear back after making a business or marriage proposal.
Most of the waiting we do is probably the uncertain kind.

But waiting for God's promise is eagerly expecting a future event
that is absolutely certain. An eager expectation that what God has

promised will happen.

It is not surprising that the two key Hebrew verbs that English versions translate "wait" can also be translated "hope," depending on the context. This is because there is a significant overlap between the two concepts. They both indicate an eager expectation of a certain future event.

The Biblical notion of hope is quite different from ours. The English word "hope" almost always refers to a future event that may or may not happen. When someone says, "I hope so," they mean, "It is my wish that it turns out the way I want, but I don't know if it will." As in, "I hope I get that job." Or "I hope she says yes."

But in the Scriptures the word "hope" refers to waiting for a future event that is certain. As in Titus 2:13: "[We are] waiting for our blessed hope, the appearing of the glory of our great God and Savior Jesus Christ."

Second, waiting for God to do what he's promised is *active* waiting, rather than an inert or passive waiting. The one waiting continues to seek and pray to God (e.g., Lamentations 3:25 in Chapter 2). The person waiting also does what they can think to do. Because they don't know whether or to what extent God's fulfillment of his promise includes their efforts (see "What are You Waiting For?" below).

Notice, though, that I wrote, "The person waiting *does what they can think to do.*" That is all that God or anyone can ask. After all, in anything we wait for—or in any endeavor for that matter—there is always more we could have done. All we need concern ourselves with is doing what we, or others we trust, can think to do.

Waiting is Suffering

Waiting for God to do what he's promised is hard. No, strike that. Waiting for God is its own kind of suffering. Especially when what God has promised is something we desperately or urgently need.

It's always been that way. But it poses a special challenge for those of us raised in an instant-gratification culture. Who expect everything to come to us quickly or easily. The attitude that technology has aided and abetted.

Our culture has little tolerance for waiting. "Waiting is for fools," says the culture. "Waiting is being inactive, reactive and passive! You must be proactive if you want to succeed in this world!"

But in any culture or any age, waiting for God has always been a severe test of our faith. Why? Because while we wait, and try to make sense out of why it is taking so long, all kinds of tormenting thoughts run through our minds, exacerbating the difficulty.

For example, we tell ourselves that if God was going to answer our prayer as he'd promised, he would have done it by now. He obviously has said no, or changed his mind. This "If God was going to do it, he would have done it by now" thinking is extremely common. And it commonly leads to giving up and missing out on the blessing.

Some of us worry that the reason that God hasn't fulfilled his promise is because we have done something to offend or disappoint him.

In our lowest moments, we wonder if there is anyone there.

In Chapter 2 we read the promise, "Cast your burden on the LORD and he will sustain you." For me, waiting for God to keep his promise is a burden that gets heavier the longer the promise goes unfulfilled. A burden that threatens to crush the faith and hope right out of you.

Because as the weeks turn into months, or the months into years, the easiest thing to do is to listen to the voice telling you that what you're waiting for will never happen. The change you've been expecting will never come. You've been waiting in vain, deluding yourself with false hope.

By the way, if you're looking for someone who is an example of waiting gracefully, don't look to me. Too often, I haven't. I've gone through the whole range of emotions while I've waited. I've raged. I've wept. I've given up and given in to hopelessness. I've concluded that there is no God. I've bottomed out. More than once.

Of course, being of northern European descent, I'm probably genetically prone to unhealthy ruminating that leads to ungraceful waiting. I can, and often do, think things to death. I tend to over-analyze everything in an attempt to figure out why something is or is not happening.

But whether you are like me or not, waiting is suffering and can be a severe test of faith. Especially when you are waiting for God to rescue you or someone you care about from some trouble or painful situation.

Article: Sometimes It Seems that God has Little Regard for Our Time-Boundness

I'm not particularly comforted by the answer that the Apostle Peter once upon a time gave to those who accused God of being slow in fulfilling his promises. "God is not slow as some count slowness. For a thousand years in his sight are as a day; and a day as a thousand years" (2 Peter 3:8). That's all well and good. But we—the ones to whom God has made his promises--are time-bound creatures whose lives are fleeting and brief.

Sometimes it seems that God gives little thought to our time-boundness. To how quickly our lives go by. To how soon we grow old. And die.

After all, what Peter said is true. God is eternal. Which means that he is without beginning or end. Which means he is not constrained by time at all. He is outside of time. He enters and exits it at will. Perhaps it is difficult for him to understand or have empathy for us poor time-bound creations.

In writing what he did Peter was drawing upon the psalm of Moses (Psalm 90). Moses said the same thing about God. Yet whereas Peter sees the contrast between our time-boundness and God's eternal nature positively, Moses views it negatively.

> You return man to dust and say, "Return, O children of man!" 4 For a thousand years in your sight are but as yesterday when it is past, or as a watch in the night. 5 You sweep them away as with a flood; they are like a dream, like grass that is renewed in the morning: 6 in the morning it flourishes and is renewed; in the evening it fades and withers. . . . The years of our life are seventy, or even by reason of strength eighty; yet their span is but toil and trouble; they are soon gone, and we fly away. . . . Return, O LORD! How long? Have pity on your servants! 14 Satisfy us in the morning with your steadfast love, that we may rejoice and be glad all our days. 15 Make us glad for as many days as you have afflicted us, and for as many years as we have seen evil.

Moses wrote this at some point during the 40 years that the nation of Israel wandered in the wilderness, before they were allowed to enter the "Promise Land." His argument is, "God I know you are eternal, but remember that we aren't! We are time-bound, and our time on this earth is so fleeting. And what little life we have often involves suffering. So take pity on us time-bound creatures and at long last, keep your promise, and let us enter the land you promised to Abraham, Isaac and Jacob."

Moses wasn't alone in his complaint. David wrote Psalm 39 when he was going through suffering of some kind that he interpreted as God's disciplining him. In the midst of that suffering he felt the need to remind God of his time-boundness: "You have made my days a mere handbreadth; the span of my years is as nothing before you. Each man's life is but a breath" (39:5). At the very end of the psalm David cries out to God, "Look away from me, that I may smile again, before I depart and am no more" (39:13)!

As you can see, I'm not alone in my observation that sometimes it seems that God gives little thought to our finiteness. To how quickly our lives go by. To how soon we grow old. And die.

But it isn't so. God does care. How do I know? Because God's eternal Son became man. The Word became flesh and dwelt among us. The timeless willingly became time-bound. Jesus Christ does understand what it is to be time-bound. He knows what it is like to see life race by. He has first-hand experience. He gets it. He experienced life in time. He experienced its fleetingness.

Jesus also has experienced needing particular things "in season" and "at the right time." He knows that help can come too late. That our livelihood--and even our lives themselves--can depend on help coming in time--before it is too late.

He knows all about aging. He gets that too. He is fully aware that if too much time passes, we might not be able to enjoy or even use the promised blessings.

But he also understands that not everything promised can be given immediately. Not everything promised should be given immediately. Even if it can be.

God always has a good reason for being "slow" in fulfilling his promises. It always is for our good. In our moments of exasperation it may appear that because he is timeless, God forgets that we aren't. But it only appears that way. God became incarnate in the person of Jesus Christ. He gets our time-boundness. He cares.

Waiting is Worship

When it comes to waiting, thankfully, it isn't all bad news. In fact, when we continue to believe that God will keep his promises to us, despite the painful delay, it pleases God immensely.

Martin Luther went so far as to assert that waiting for God is worshiping God; in fact, it is the best and truest worship.

> Reason dreams that God has to be worshiped and appeased with physical sacrifices or other exercises devised by men. But the examples of the fathers show that the foremost and best worship is to wait for God.
>
> . . . These very noble examples are presented to us in the saintly men in order that we may learn that the main and spiritual worship of God does not consist in building temples and proliferating ceremonies. All these are childish amusements through which God attracts and invites us to Himself, as He used to exercise the Jews by means of various rites and by a kind of pedagogy, as it were. But the worship of the fathers is a waiting.
>
> . . . Consequently, God must be worshiped with faith, hope, and love. Outward ceremonies are merely exercises for the unlearned by means of which they are accustomed to the far loftier duties of godliness, just as infants are first nourished with milk and softer food. But we who govern and teach others should learn that the true worship of God does not consist in sacrificing cattle, etc., but in holding fast to His promise and believing that it is true and unfailing. This trust is followed by the hope which reminds me that I should wait and that I have a gracious God (Martin Luther, "Lectures on Genesis: Chapters 21-25, AE:320-321, 322-323).

Luther held that waiting for God is the truest worship because, for him, trusting God's promises was at the heart of Christian worship. In worship, God promises us his grace and we receive that grace through faith.

Waiting for God to keep his promises, then, is simply faith that hangs on and refuses to give up. It is faith that keeps on believing until the bitter end that God most certainly will do for us what he has promised. All the great saints of old worshiped God in this way.

As Jeremiah puts it, "It is good that one should wait quietly for the deliverance of the LORD" (Lam 3:26). It is good indeed! Few things please God more than worship such as this.

Example: God Promised Abraham Descendants

One of the best known examples of how God goes about keeping his promises is the promise he made to Abraham. The promise that Abraham—though he was currently childless—would have a multitude of descendants. It is a famous example demonstrating that God is wont to delay the fulfilling of his promises (from our perspective), so that we are forced to wait.

Genesis records that when God first made this promise, Abraham was 75 years old (Genesis 12:2-4). It also records that a son wasn't born to Sarah, his wife, until 25 long years later. Abraham was 100 when Isaac was born. (Genesis 21:1-5).

If God had told Abraham when he first made the promise that it was going to take 25 years, perhaps it would have been easier. But he didn't. God gave no indication how long it would take. At any point along the way.

Also, given that this was the very first promise that God had made to Abraham, the patriarch had no frame of reference or experience to draw from. Since he was already 75 years old, it would have been reasonable for Abraham to assume that the promise would be fulfilled sooner rather than later. It wasn't sooner.

Ten years went by and Abraham was still childless. Believing that God would keep his promise—but confused that he hadn't—Sarah got the idea that though Abraham was indeed to be the father, perhaps she wasn't meant to be the mother.

So she gave Hagar, her Egyptian slave, to Abraham, and gave him permission to have a child through her. The slave conceived, and a son, Ishmael, was born. After the birth, as far as we know, there was no further word from God on the subject—for 13 more years. So the couple must have concluded that Ishmael was the promised son.

But when Abraham was 99, God appeared to him and blessed him again, repeating his promise that he would have a multitude of descendants. Then, in a surprising turn, God told Abraham that a son would be born to Sarah, and that kings and nations would descend from her.

Abraham's reaction? He fell on his face and laughed. He thought to himself, "Shall I have a son when I am 100, and shall Sarah be a mother at 90?" God wasn't laughing. He clarified that the promise he had made 24 years before was going to be fulfilled through a son that would be born to Sarah (Genesis 17:15-21). Nine months later, Isaac was born (Genesis 21).

I relate this in detail to show the reader that it was certainly not easy for Abraham and Sarah to have waited all this time. As we would have done, they struggled over the delay. They were confused. They tried to figure it out. They thought that they needed to help God fulfill it and concocted the Hagar plan (which God blessed nonetheless). Then for 13 years they probably didn't give it much thought, because they assumed that Ishmael had been the fulfillment of the promise.

In the end, though, God faithfully kept his promise, though in a totally unexpected way. 90 year old Sarah gave birth to Isaac. But it took a long, long time.

Example: Like Father, Like Son – The Promise to Isaac

Another example that God can take a frustratingly long time to fulfill a promise involved Abraham's son, Isaac and Isaac's wife, Rebecca. They too had to wait a long time before their firstborn came.

Whereas the story of the giving and fulfillment of God's promise of a son to Abraham spans 9 chapters in the book of Genesis, the story of Isaac's wait is told in a few verses. Because it is so quickly told it is easy to miss it. Only the bare facts are given.

Genesis records that Isaac was 40 when he married Rebecca. In the very next verse we are told that "Isaac prayed to the LORD for his wife, because she was barren. And the LORD granted his prayer, and Rebekah his wife conceived" (Genesis 25:21).

The impression is given that Rebecca must have been childless for a very short time. The story goes on to tell us that Rebecca gave birth to twins, who were named Esau and Jacob. Only at the very end of this account do we find out that Isaac was 60 when the twin boys were born (Genesis 25:26)!

So like father, like son. Isaac also was made to wait a very long time before the promise was fulfilled. 20 years to be exact.

Half the Difficulty of Waiting . . .

As the Abraham example illustrated, half the difficulty of waiting is that we have no idea how long it is going to take. If when God first made the promise to Abraham he had given him some idea of how long it would be, the waiting would have been easier.

If God had said to Abraham, "I want to make it very clear that your promised son won't be born for many, many years," it would been less difficult. Or if at any point during the 25 year wait, God had given an idea of how long, it would have been easier to be patient.

Unfortunately, not only did God not give Abraham an idea of how long—he said nothing at all for over ten years. During that time God was completely silent. Leaving Abraham and Sarah to wonder, "Did we misunderstand God's promise? Did we imagine it all? Has he changed his mind? Are we supposed to be doing something? Has something we've done angered him?"

Not knowing how long, and experiencing excruciatingly long periods of silence, is half the struggle for us too. It leads us to ask the same kinds of soul-searching questions.

What are You Waiting For?

Occasionally, we may be waiting when we shouldn't be. In this next section I'd like to discuss scenarios where that may be the case.

You Shouldn't Be Waiting Because What God Promised You Already Happened

Sometimes what God promised you already happened. And somehow you missed it. Obviously, in such a case you shouldn't be waiting.

Missed it? Really? Yes. It can happen. Usually the reason we miss the fulfillment of God's promise is there was a big mismatch between our expectations and God's chosen method. We had pictured beforehand exactly how God was going to fulfill his promise to us. So when it happened in a way we hadn't expected, we missed it.

Whether we realize it or not, many of us typically expect God to fulfill his promises in ways that are *obvious*, *immediate* and *direct*.

By *obvious*, I mean we expect him to do it in a way that is practically impossible to miss. We are predisposed to expect God to keep his promises in obvious ways, because in the Bible God often did it that way. Obvious miracles. Obvious answers to prayer. Obvious fulfillment of promises and prophesies. That kind of thing.

By *immediate*, I mean we expect God to fulfill his promises now. Right away. Instantaneously. Or at least quickly and speedily.

By *direct*, I mean we expect the fulfillment to come directly from God to us with no intermediaries in between. God just "zaps" us directly. Or miraculously.

For example, we ask God to strengthen us as he has promised. We expect him to do it directly, infusing us with new strength.

Instead God fulfills the promise through a fellow Christian who contacts us and in some way encourages us. Or perhaps we find ourselves in a position in which we have to encourage someone else, even though we may think we have nothing to give, and it is the last thing we want to do. But in that activity we ourselves are strengthened. Or God fulfills it by leading us to overhear something, see something or read something that strengthens us.

In other words, he kept his promise to strengthen us, but he did it indirectly, through intermediaries.

If we expect what God has promised to always happen in ways that are obvious, immediate and direct, we are setting ourselves up to miss the fulfillment when it comes. It isn't that he doesn't work that way. It is that he frequently does not work in obvious, immediate and direct ways.

The quintessential Biblical example of this is the way God fulfilled the promise of the coming Messiah. Beginning in Genesis, and throughout the Old Testament with increasing clarity and specificity, God promised to send the Messiah who would save his people and defeat their enemies.

Yet when God fulfilled the promise and the Messiah came in the person of Jesus of Nazareth, many didn't recognize it. And when they were told Jesus was the one, they refused to believe it. Why? Because the Messiah they expected was not the Messiah they got. Even though in every particular he was and did what God had promised the Messiah would be and do.

They expected him to be a mighty military leader. He was a carpenter. They expected that he would be born from obvious descendants of King David in Jerusalem. He was born to unknown parents in a stable in Bethlehem. He was from Galilee. He wasn't physically impressive, etc. The last straw for many was when he was executed on the cross as a criminal.

In fact, Jesus was so at odds with contemporary expectations of how God's promise of a Messiah would be fulfilled, that even John the Baptist, the very one who first publicly introduced Jesus as the Messiah, began to have doubts. He sent his disciples to Jesus to double-check that he was indeed the Messiah (Matthew 11:2-6).

So if the way God chose to fulfill his most significant promise was missed by the vast majority, because it didn't match their expectations, should it be surprising if the same thing sometimes happens to us?

Assembly Required

Some things we buy have "No Assembly Required" stamped on the box. Which is always welcome news because then we know the purchased product is ready for use right away. Nothing more is required of us. Easy. Simplicity itself.

Unfortunately there are some products we buy that are "Assembly Required." The good news with assembly required products is that we do have the complete product. All the parts are included. But before we can use the product we have to do some assembling.

I'm convinced that one common reason that we miss God's fulfillment of his promise to us is because it comes marked "Assembly Required." Which flies in the face of what we typically expect. We expect the fulfilled promises or answered prayers to be easy. Finished. Complete. Ready to use.

When God fulfills a promise "Assembly Required" it is fulfilled. The prayer is already answered. What he promised was truly given. He has given us the box with all the pieces in it. We actually have in our possession everything we asked for. But there remains some assembling for us to do before we can fully enjoy the benefits or use of what was given.

There are many Biblical examples of assembly required.

A good Old Testament example is the Promised Land. When Joshua and the people crossed the Jordan River and first stepped foot in Canaan, at that moment the promise was fulfilled. Given. But some assembling was required before they could fully enjoy the benefits of that promise. They had to conquer the peoples who already lived there. They had to divide up the land into twelve territories for the twelve tribes of Israel. Only then could they fully enjoy the fulfilled promise.

Then there is the example of Naaman, the commander of the Syrian army, recorded in 2 Kings 5. He had leprosy. He learned that Elisha the prophet could heal someone with leprosy. So he made the long trek to the prophet's house in Israel with a large retinue in tow.

But when he knocked on the door, instead of Elisha himself coming to the door and dramatically healing him, Elisha's servant came to the door with this message from the prophet: "Go wash yourself in the Jordan River seven times, and your flesh will be restored to you."

When Naaman heard this he said,

> "Behold, I thought that he would surely come out to me and stand and call upon the name of the LORD his God, and wave his hand over the place and cure the leper. [12] Are not Abana and Pharpar, the rivers of Damascus, better than all the waters of Israel? Could I not wash in them and be clean?" So he turned and went away in a rage" (2 Kings 5:11-12).

What was Naaman's problem? Why did he get so angry? He felt

slighted that Elisha himself didn't come out, sure. But part of it was that he was expecting a no assembly required healing. He was expecting it to be easy and immediate. Instead he was told, in effect, "First there is some assembling you have to do – go dip yourself in the Jordan River seven times – then you will receive the full benefit of what you asked."

Another example is Christ's healing of ten lepers, recorded in Luke 17. They pleaded with Jesus to heal them. And he did. But he required them to do some assembling. He said, "'Go and show yourselves to the priests.' And as they went they were cleansed" (Luke 17:24). He answered their prayer. But they had to do some assembling: They had to go show themselves to the priests as the Mosaic Law required.

Here is a contemporary example. Someone prays for a job. Then they discover a job opportunity but to fully take advantage of it, they have to train or retrain. Or they have to take classes or learn a new craft. It isn't something they've done before. It isn't at all the kind of job they were expecting or assuming. Until they start their new vocation or get hired they can't fully enjoy the fruits of it. But all the pieces are in the box. What the person asked has been given. But to actually enjoy the benefits of the finished product, he has to assemble the pieces into the finished product. He has to do the training or take the classes, etc.

Or let's say someone asked for healing. If God answered "No Assembly Required," the person would be healed easily, perhaps with only one doctor's visit, or one prescription filled.

If instead God gave an assembly required answer then the person would need more doctor's visits, perhaps. Or they might have to try a number of different things in order to fully realize the healing. All the pieces of the healing were in the box from the beginning. But he had to do the assembling.

Because we sometimes miss the fact that what God promised has already happened, we do unnecessary waiting and cause ourselves unnecessary misery. And we miss his fulfillment because we assumed that the fulfilled promise would be easy, requiring nothing more of us at all.

God May Be Waiting for You to Do *Something*

Another possible reason you shouldn't be waiting is because God is waiting for you to do something.

I went back and forth about even putting this section in the book. I decided to because occasionally what is holding things up is not "God's timetable" but you. Specifically, God hasn't fulfilled his promise to you because something you are supposed to do is an integral part of God acting on your behalf. That something is like the first domino in a line of dominos. Once it falls the rest fall. But until it falls, nothing happens.

There are several inescapable examples in the Bible that convince me that there are times that we have to do something before God will answer our prayer. Here are two of them.

David, the Madman

The first example involves David. Psalm 34 is one of David's best known psalms. In it he celebrates how God delivered him when he prayed to him.

> I sought the LORD, and he answered me and delivered me from all my fears. [5] Those who look to him are radiant, and their faces shall never be ashamed. [6] This poor man cried, and the LORD heard him and saved him out of all his troubles (4-6).

At the end of the psalm, David encourages the rest of us to do what he did. To ask God to deliver us. When we do, he promises us that God will deliver us just as God delivered him.

> When the righteous cry for help, the LORD hears and delivers them out of all their troubles. [18] The LORD is near to the brokenhearted and saves the crushed in spirit. [19] Many are the afflictions of the righteous, but the LORD delivers him out of them all (17-19).

Perhaps it's just me, but David gives the impression that all he did was pray to God for deliverance, and God did it all without any further involvement on David's part. But that wasn't the case.

How do we know? Because Psalm 34 includes a preface which gives us the historical setting of the psalm. It tells us what inspired David to write it. It says, *"Of David, when he changed his behavior before Abimelech, so that he drove him out, and he went away."*

The preface is referencing an incident in David's life that happened before he became king. At a time when King Saul was pursuing him all over Israel in order to kill him. The story is told in full in 1 Samuel 21.

To escape Saul, in an act of desperation, David fled to Gath, a city of the Philistines--bitter enemies of Israel--to seek protection in the king's household. Not the best idea. Because when David arrived, the king's servants recognized him and told the king who he was.

When David discovered he had been found out, he was terrified. He decided to pretend that he was a madman: "So he changed his behavior before them and pretended to be insane in their hands and made marks on the doors of the gate and let his spittle run down his beard.". The king was fooled by David's act and said to his servants, "Do I lack madmen that you allow this man to play madman in my presence? Why have you brought him into my house?" David was summarily dismissed and he escaped.

So what do we learn from this? We learn that, though David obviously cried out to God to rescue him from such a perilous situation, he didn't just pray and sit back and wait for God to act. He did something. He used his brain. He came up with a plan. He executed the plan.

David was right in seeing that God answered his prayer and delivered him. Because God was working through it all.

Notice that the "something" David did wasn't exactly brilliant. It was rather stupid, actually. To pretend to be crazy was a very risky thing to do. The chances of it turning out very badly were considerable. But the point here is that David did something. And that something was part of God's answer to David's prayer.

Joseph's "Something"

I reference the amazing story of Joseph in several places throughout the book. It certainly is a pivotal example of how God sometimes goes about fulfilling his promises (read his story in Genesis 37, 39-50).

But here I want to point out that before he was set free and elevated to lordship over all Egypt, Joseph did something. Several things. If he hadn't done them, it is unlikely that the story would have turned out the same.

At some point after Joseph had been thrown into prison, Pharaoh threw two of his own servants—his chief cupbearer and the chief baker—into the same prison, until he decided what to do with them. They each had a dream on the same night. The next morning, they were troubled about it, and Joseph noticed it. So he did something. He did two things.

The first thing he did was to take an interest in these two servants. He didn't have to do this. He could have seen that they were troubled about something and ignored them. He had problems of his own, after all. But he took an interest in them and asked them why they were so down. They told him about the dreams.

That led to the second thing Joseph did. He offered to interpret their dreams for them, and did so. He told the cupbearer that his dream meant that in three days Pharaoh would let him out of prison and restore him to his position. Then he told the baker that, unfortunately, his dream meant that in three days Pharaoh would let him out of prison and cut off his head!

That done, Joseph asked the cupbearer to be so kind as to mention him to Pharaoh when he got out of prison. Unfortunately the cupbearer forgot to do that. For two long years.

What jogged his memory two years later was that Pharaoh himself had a disturbing dream. Two in fact. And no one could interpret them. The cupbearer then remembered Joseph and told Pharaoh about him. Joseph was summoned to court and interpreted Pharaoh's dreams. Joseph told him that God was revealing to Pharaoh that there would be seven years of great plenty in Egypt followed by seven years of terrible famine.

Now came the third "something" Joseph did. Having interpreted the dreams, he offered some unasked for advice. He advised Pharaoh to select a wise man to put in charge of stockpiling grain during the years of plenty and distributing the grain during the years of famine. Pharaoh liked the idea, and said, "Who is wiser than you, Joseph?" So he chose Joseph.

If Joseph hadn't done the first two things, he wouldn't have interpreted the cupbearer's dream. And if he hadn't done so, the cupbearer would never have thought of Joseph when Pharaoh had his own dreams. Joseph would not have been brought before Pharaoh.

If Joseph hadn't done the third thing, Pharaoh almost certainly would have let him go free. But it is unlikely that at that very moment it would have occurred to him to select an overseer to stockpile and distribute the grain. Making it possible that he wouldn't have chosen Joseph.

It was all part of God's amazing plan, of course. It was the way he chose to answer Joseph's prayer and keep his promises. But Joseph did several "somethings" that were an integral part of God's deliverance. Deliverance that might not have happened if Joseph hadn't done his somethings.

A Concluding Thought

One final comment on this. The reason I hesitated including the "What Are You Waiting For?" section is because in most cases we are supposed to be waiting for God to act on our behalf. The wait has to do with God's method of promise-keeping, not us.

But as we wait we torment ourselves unnecessarily with thoughts like, "What if the reason nothing has happened is because I'm not being proactive enough, haven't tried hard enough, or haven't worked harder or smarter?" Or "What if God has repeatedly tried to help me but I keep frustrating his help by my self-defeating ways, etc.?" Which is all unnecessary torment.

The only reason I included this section is to encourage you to make sure that, as you are waiting, you do what you can think to do to resolve the situation. It doesn't have to be brilliant. It doesn't have to take a lot of thought. But do whatever you can think to do. Because the something you do may be an integral part of God of keeping his promise and helping you.

But if you have done what you can think to do, or what trusted advisors can think to do, and nothing has come from it, then it is highly likely that God is telling you to wait.

God May Be Waiting for You to Repent

> "Knowing this first of all, that scoffers will come in the last days with scoffing, following their own sinful desires. 4 They will say, "Where is the promise of his coming? For ever since the fathers fell asleep, all things are continuing as they were from the beginning of creation" (2 Peter 3:3-4).

The promise Peter has in mind is that of Christ's second coming. Though in a derivative sense it can apply to any promise.

The "scoffers" Peter mentions were ridiculing the promise of Christ's Second Coming as a false or delusional promise. They were interpreting Christ's "no show" after so many years as proof that it was a false promise to begin with.

Aren't we tempted to reach the same conclusion when whatever God has promised appears to be a "no show" after a long time? There is a scoffer inside every one of us who points to a seemingly unfulfilled promise as proof that none of it is true.

But the Apostle Peter tells his readers that isn't the reason at all. There is another reason altogether why the fulfillment of God's promise sometimes goes unfulfilled for a long time. The truth, Peter tells them, is that the reason they are waiting for God's promise is that he's been waiting for them. He's been waiting for them to repent.

> "The Lord is not slow to fulfill his promise as some count slowness, but is patient toward you, not wishing that any should perish, but that all should reach repentance." (2 Peter 3:9).

Now I know that talking about repentance is a real downer. It gives off so much negative energy and all. But I would be irresponsible if I didn't point out that sometimes the reason that God hasn't yet fulfilled his promise to us is that there is something that we need to repent of first.

And that something we need to repent of should be fairly obvious. It shouldn't be something we have to ransack our brains to find. It shouldn't be something that only doing an extensive personal inventory will reveal.

It probably involves some behavior that is obviously not Christian. That has pricked our conscience more than once. That someone has brought to our attention, perhaps. That in our hearts we know is wrong, but we don't want to give it up. Or we don't want to make the lifestyle change we know we should. So we've put it off. Or we've defended and justified it.

But unless we give it up or make the change, and receive forgiveness through Christ, God will not fulfill his promise to us.

Do we really expect God to keep his promises to us when we are obviously living contrary to his will? If God did so he would risk being an enabler of sinful behavior, potentially keeping us in it. Putting us at risk of ultimately falling from grace altogether. Something God would never, ever do.

Speaking of risk, putting a section in the book about how impenitence can keep God from fulfilling his promise, is risking tormenting my sensitive readers. Perhaps you.

I say "tormenting" because Christians with overly sensitive consciences are prone to constantly see sin in themselves when God sees none. When these Christians hear that impenitence may be a reason that the answer to their prayer hasn't come yet, they immediately conclude, "That's me!" They reach that conclusion because they see all too clearly how they fall short of being the perfect Christian they think they should be. So they investigate every nook and cranny of their lives, probing their thoughts, words, deeds and motives—agonizing over the realization that there is so much sin in them, that it could be anything.

If that describes you then I can guarantee that this section has nothing to do with you. It is not about you or for you. There is nothing to see here. Move along!

In fact, I believe that impenitence is seldom the reason why what God has promised hasn't happened yet. But because it sometimes is, I included it here.

CHAPTER FIVE – GOD'S METHOD OF KEEPING HIS PROMISES: PART II

The concept that God requires us to wait before he fulfills his promises is fairly well known.

There is another part of God's method of promise-keeping, however, that isn't. But it is critical that you know it. In fact, knowing it is often the difference between receiving what God has promised and not receiving it. Not knowing it can lead to profound disillusionment and doubt.

And it is this: God sometimes allows our lives to go from bad to worse before what he promised happens. And in some cases he allows the exact opposite of what he has promised to happen.

A Different Kind of Suffering

I think most Christians know that they will suffer in this life. They know that, in the words of Jesus, "In the world you will have tribulation" (John 16:33).

I hope you know that most of our tribulations are not a sign that we've done something wrong. Rather, God permits suffering in our lives for our good. To make us better Christians.

I knew all that, too. But what I experienced and what this chapter is about was a different sort of suffering. Something new. Something I hadn't previously encountered.

What was new was the interplay between God's promises and suffering. That when we are eagerly waiting for something God has promised to happen, sometimes the exact opposite of what he promised happens instead. Or at the very least, our lives noticeably worsen.

It is almost as if the more we believe that what God has promised will happen, the worse our lives get. Or the more we pray, the worse off we become.

Here is an example. We ask God for some specific need. On the basis of his many promises of prayer we expect to receive it. We wait. It doesn't happen. Then, seemingly adding insult to injury, while we're waiting all kinds of problems arise in our lives. Adversity. Troubles. Setbacks. Loss. Sometimes—shockingly--the exact opposite of what we asked happens.

So we try to make sense out of it. Inevitably we reach the most "obvious" conclusion that God is saying no to our prayer. But it's more than that. It's almost as if what we asked has angered God. Or as if something in our lives really has displeased him. Why else would all the bad things be happening? Why else would our lives seem less blessed by him than before? Why else would it seem that we are cursed? Even darker questions cloud our minds.

In my case, I had been unemployed for 18 months. I had asked God to lead me to a job. Not only did he not give it, but the bottom dropped out in other areas of my life. Things went from bad to worse. I was staring poverty in the face.

I was bewildered and angry. Why was God doing this to me? I hadn't asked for something extravagant or forbidden. I had asked for something I needed. A basic necessity. Yet, not only was he refusing me, not only did it seem that he was ignoring me, but it almost seemed that he was against me; or that he hated me.

I had no frame of reference to deal with this. I couldn't remember anything in the Bible that explained it. I'd never heard of anyone else experiencing it. I had never preached on it, nor had I heard another pastor talk about it. So I took it personally and began to wonder if it was just me.

An Injection of Hope

Then one day as I was reading, I stumbled upon something that grabbed me by the ears. As I read it, it was like someone had just pumped pure hope into my bloodstream.

It was the place in Martin Luther's Romans Commentary where he was interpreting Romans 8:26. Romans 8:26 says, "Likewise the Spirit helps us in our weakness. For we do not know what to pray for as we ought, but the Spirit himself intercedes for us with groanings too deep for words."

Here is what Luther wrote. Pay attention to the first, third and fifth paragraphs especially:

> It is not a bad sign, but a very good one, if things seem to turn out contrary to our requests. Just as it is not a good sign if everything turns out favorably for our requests.

> The reason is that the excellence of God's counsel and will are far above our counsel and will, as Is. 55:8–9 says: "For My thoughts are not your thoughts, neither are your ways My ways, says the Lord. For as the heavens are higher than the earth, so are My ways higher than your ways and My thoughts than your thoughts."

> . . . Hence it results that when we pray to God for something, whatever these things may be, and He hears our prayers and begins to give us what we wish, He gives in such a way that He contravenes all of our conceptions, that is, our ideas, so that He may seem to us to be more offended after our prayers and to do less after we have asked than He did before. And He does all this because it is the nature of God first to destroy and tear down whatever is in us before He gives us His good things, as the Scripture says: "The Lord makes poor and makes rich, He brings down to hell and raises up" (1 Sam. 2:7, 6).

> . . . Therefore, when everything is hopeless for us and all things begin to go against our prayers and desires, then those unutterable groans begin. And then "the Spirit helps us in our weakness" (Rom. 8:26). For unless the Spirit were helping, it would be impossible for us to bear this action of God by which He hears us and accomplishes what we pray for. Then the soul is told: "Be strong, wait for the Lord, and let your heart take courage and bear up under God" (Ps. 27:14). And again: "Be subject to the Lord and pray to Him," "and He will act" (Ps. 37:7, 5).

> . . . But those who have the Spirit are helped by Him. Thus they do not lose hope but have confidence, even though they are aware of what goes contrary to what they have so sincerely prayed for. For the work of God must be hidden and never understood, even when it happens. But it is never hidden in any other way than under that which appears contrary to our

conceptions and ideas. (Martin Luther, "Lectures on Romans," AE 25:364-367).

A couple of things in this Luther passage were of great help to me.

First, he was describing exactly what I had experienced. That God sometimes does allow the opposite of what we've asked to happen. He does allow our lives to worsen while we are waiting for him to answer our prayers. So perhaps God wasn't singling me out after all. What I was going through did not mean that God was unhappy with me.

Second, and most importantly to me, Luther claimed that the fact that the opposite of what I had asked had happened did not mean that God had said no to my prayer. Doing the exact opposite was simply the way that God had chosen to give me what I asked. It was all part of the strange way that God goes about fulfilling his promises to us.

As much as I respect Martin Luther, I wasn't just going to take his word for it. So when I subsequently began to search the Scriptures, I was delighted to find the same teaching there. Or, I should say, I found examples of it there. In the stories of Joseph, David, Mary & Martha, and others. Stories where those who were waiting for what God promised to happen--or were waiting for him to give them what they asked--experienced the exact opposite instead (read about it later in this chapter).

A More Jarring Suffering

Let me repeat that I was quite familiar with the Biblical teaching that all Christians will suffer in this life. And that God permits it for our good to make us better Christians. I've experienced that kind of suffering many times in my life, as I'm sure you have.

But this new suffering was far more jarring to me. When you're eagerly waiting for God to do what he promised, and desperately need him to, but the opposite happens instead, it shakes your faith. Because it appears to give the lie to God's promises. It calls into question everything you've believed about God.

Many Christians have never noticed any of this. I think it is because the only ones who notice are those who have some great need; and they go to God with that need, fully expecting him to answer their prayer and provide for them, as he has promised to do.

The truth is, many Christians don't ever need God. They are so well off or have so many safety nets in place, that even when they have some great need, they don't need God. Plus there are so many human helpers out there to give us what we need. Who needs God?

Another sad truth is that many Christians don't expect God to do what he has promised. Countless Christians *have* experienced praying to God for something and having the opposite happen. But it isn't nearly as spiritually jarring to them, I think, because, first of all, they didn't pray with God's promises of prayer in mind. Second of all, they didn't expect God to keep those promises of prayer. Their attitude wasn't "God is definitely going to give me this because he has specifically promised to do so in the Bible." It was, "I hope God gives me what I asked, but it's up to him. He might but he might not."

So when the opposite of what they ask happens, they just conclude that what they asked wasn't God's will. Or they figure that they must have prayed incorrectly, etc. So it disappoints them. It saddens them. But it isn't jarring to their faith.

The Most Difficult Faith

One last Luther quotation, which beautifully captures what I have learned about the way God fulfills his promises. It comes from his lectures on the book of Genesis. In it he takes a moment to reflect on different aspects of faith that are challenging.

> For faith first carries us away into things that are invisible when it points out that things that are not apparent to the eye must be accepted. This we can somehow bear and put up with. The heart, however, is not only led into what is invisible; but it is also kept in suspense and is put off for a long time, just as Abraham, as has been stated above, waited for 25 years before a son was born to him, and Isaac is without offspring for 20 years. **But the third and by far the most serious thing is experienced when delay and postponement are followed by a disposition to the opposite effect.** It is then that he who is able to endure and wait, to hope for the things that are being delayed, and to be pleased with what is contrary, will eventually learn from experience that God is truthful and keeps His promises. (Martin Luther, "Lectures on Genesis: Chapters 21-25," AE 4:321; emphasis mine)

"But the third and by far the most serious thing," writes the reformer, is when waiting a long time for God to fulfill his promise is followed by the exact opposite of what he's promised happening. However, the one who can endure it, and can continue to hope and believe, "will eventually learn from experience that God is truthful and keeps his promises." And he does!

P. Bucher

Mary, Martha and Lazarus

One of the best known of Christ's miracles is the raising of Lazarus from the dead, recorded in John 11. In John's Gospel, the raising of Lazarus was the last and greatest of Jesus' "signs"-- miracles that Jesus performed to reveal himself as the Christ and Son of God.

What is less known is what happened before the miracle. How the story began.

Jesus and his disciples had recently left Jerusalem and Judea because the Jewish leaders wanted to stone him to death for what they considered to be blasphemy. They traveled somewhere to the east of the Jordan River, where John the Baptist had begun his prophetic ministry. They were there long enough that "many believed in him there" (John 10:22-42).

While there, someone arrived with a message from two sisters named Mary and Martha, who along with their brother Lazarus, were special friends of Jesus. The message brought dire news: "Lord, be aware that he whom you love is sick" (John 11:1-3).

The nature of Lazarus's sickness is unknown to us. But it must have been serious for the sisters to have dispatched such a messenger. Mary, Martha and Lazarus lived in the village of Bethany which was about 2 miles south of Jerusalem. Jesus and his disciples were about a 2-3 day journey away.

What happened next is almost inexplicable. Here is how John puts it: "Now Jesus loved Martha and her sister and Lazarus. So, when he heard that Lazarus was ill, he stayed two days longer in the place where he was" (John 11:5-6).

Really? Jesus loved Martha, Mary and Lazarus. So when he heard that Lazarus was ill, *he stayed where he was for two more days?* What kind of love is that?

The three siblings were like family to Jesus. They were very dear to him. Almost anyone else, upon learning that someone dear to them was seriously ill, would have immediately departed, frantically hurried, taken the quickest route, and chosen the fastest method of travel in order to reach their sick loved one in time. But Jesus—in one of the most counter-intuitive moves imaginable—stayed put for two days longer.

This was totally uncharacteristic of Jesus. Hardly a day went by that he didn't heal dozens of sick people immediately, as soon as they asked or presented the need. But now, after hearing that someone that was especially dear to him was dangerously sick, not only did he do nothing—he intentionally did the opposite of what anyone would have expected him to do.

Jesus knew what he was doing, though. He had a plan.

But on the surface of it, his peculiar action just seemed heartless. Cold. Unfeeling.

He loved them. He had the power to instantaneously help them. He could have left immediately and reached Lazarus in time. He could have healed him instantly from where he was without going anywhere. Instead, he chose to do nothing and wait for two whole days longer.

Jesus just let Lazarus die. He did the exact opposite of what the sisters had asked.

This lay heavily on the sisters' hearts when Jesus did arrive. Both sisters, one after the other, first Martha and later Mary, said the identical sorrowful words to him: "Lord, if you had been here, my brother would not have died." They were devastatingly disappointed.

The questions behind those words, the questions that haunted them, were, "Why didn't you come at once? Why did you let him die? Why didn't you do what we asked? Why did you allow the opposite of what we hoped for to happen? Don't you love us? Were we wrong to think you did? Have we done something to turn you against us?"

What their beloved Teacher had done floored them because it was so utterly unlike him. He had always showed himself to be so loving and good. But this, this seemed cruel.

What Jesus did made no earthly sense.

It made perfect heavenly sense, though. As they were about to discover.

As I said above, Jesus had a plan. A very good plan. A plan far above any the sisters could have conceived. In fact, you could almost say that the thoughts of Jesus were not their thoughts, nor were their ways his ways. As high as the heavens are above the earth so high were his thoughts above their thoughts, and his ways above their ways (Isaiah 55:8-9).

Jesus had a plan that would bring far more glory to God than what Mary and Martha had asked, and give them what they asked at the same time.

That plan, as we already know, was to raise Lazarus from the dead.

I love this account of the raising of Lazarus because it powerfully illustrates the way God sometimes chooses to fulfill his promises or answer our prayers. We cry out to him for help in our time of need, confident that he loves us and has the power to help us. Certain that he keeps his promises. Then, with great anticipation, we wait for the answer. And we wait. And wait. And wait. But no answer comes. As we wait, our situation worsens. Things go from bad to worse. And sometimes, the very opposite of what we asked happens.

When it happens, we are stunned. Staggered. None of it makes any earthly sense. And the haunting questions come and tear at our hearts. "God, why didn't you keep your promise? Why didn't you answer my prayer? You say you love me. You had the power to help me. But you didn't. The more I prayed about it, the worse my situation became. Now the opposite has happened! It seems cruel."

But just as Jesus had a far more glorious plan for Martha, Mary and Lazarus, so he has a far more glorious plan for you. He heard their prayer. It seemed that he had refused them. But in the end he did answer their prayer, and did keep his promises, but in a way and at a time that was far above their ability to understand. And far better than they could have imagined.

And . . . Jesus did it exactly the way he did because he loved them (John 11:5). It was an expression of his love, not just his wisdom.

So he will keep his promises and answer your prayer, though right now it may seem like he has refused you, and doesn't love you. Even though as you've waited your life has gotten worse. Or the opposite of what you've asked has happened. In the end he will give you what you asked, but in a far greater way and at a far better time than you could have ever conceived.

God always keeps his promises. But he reserves the right to fulfill those promises in his own marvelous way and in his own marvelous time. It may make no earthly sense to you. But it makes perfect heavenly sense to him.

Be patient. Don't stop believing. And you will see the glorious ways of God.

Article: Even Now

"But even now I know that whatever you ask from God, God will give you" (John 11:22).

Martha said this to Jesus. Immediately after she had said, "Lord, if you had been here, my brother would have not have died."

And it is just about the most impressive faith I've ever heard expressed.

"Even now."

"Even now I know."

"Lord, if you had been here, my brother would not have died. But even now I know that whatever you ask from God, God will give you."

Martha is saying, "We had hoped that as soon as you received our message, you would have rushed to be with him, and you would have healed Lazarus. But you didn't. And he died. Now our brother is dead and buried. We waited. We hoped. We prayed. But you didn't come. You didn't come.

"And now you show up, four days after he died. Our hearts are broken. We counted on you, our loving Lord, the one who loved Lazarus so much, to come to his rescue. But you didn't. You didn't even hurry to get here. In fact, it took you far longer to get here than it should have taken you. You took your time! You let him die! So our hearts are heavy with grief.

"But *even now*, even after all that's happened, even now, I know that whatever you ask God, God will give you."

What a remarkable woman! What an astonishing faith. Nothing that had happened altered her faith in Jesus. In her mind, everything she had previously known and believed about him was still true. She displayed no doubt. No disillusionment. No resentment. She still trusted him completely. Even though the very opposite of her heartfelt plea had happened and her beloved brother lay dead in a tomb. None of that shook her faith in Jesus.

Martha's faith is an example for us all. Especially whenever God has made us wait, our lives have worsened, and even the opposite of what we asked has happened. Like her, we should say to Jesus, "Even now, I believe you. Even now, even after all that has happened, I still believe that you will keep your promise to me. Even now I believe that you will give me what I asked. Even now."

David Shall be King

A well-known Bible verse is Psalm 27:14 which states, **"Wait for the LORD; be strong, and let your heart take courage; wait for the LORD!"** (Psalm 27:14). David, Israel's greatest king, wrote those words.

"Wait for the LORD" means "Keep waiting!" It means, "Wait for the LORD to do what you've asked him to do" or "Wait for the LORD to do what he has promised."

David is urging all those who are in the midst of adversity to keep waiting, to not give up and to not lose heart. He is encouraging them to not give up on God simply because a long time has passed and God has been hidden and silent during that time.

He is lighting a fire underneath all of us who have felt forsaken by God and who are ready to throw in the towel, despairing of all hope. He is saying, "Don't be weak. Be strong! Don't be cowardly. Be courageous."

Waiting and strength are related, as only the one who has been waiting for God to do something for them knows. It requires great strength and courage to wait for God to act on your behalf when you are going through real adversity and suffering. When the very opposite of what God has promised is happening.

I say this because believers can also be waiting for God in the midst of prosperity or peace. Then little or no strength or courage is needed. Neither does anyone need to command and urge them to keep waiting.

"Wait for the LORD. Be strong and courageous. Wait for the LORD" means "Don't give up hope. Don't think that God has said no or has decided not to help you. Don't interpret the excruciatingly long time that has already passed as proof of that. Keep waiting. He will come through for you. He will keep his promise. He will most certainly answer your prayer and help you."

For What did David Wait?

Someone might ask, "Who is this David to instruct the rest of us about waiting for God? For what did David have to wait?"

Oh, not much. He just had to unexpectedly wait at least ten years to become king. During that time he was the original fugitive, living in the desert, constantly avoiding capture, and running for his life. That's all.

A little backstory will fill in the blanks. We learn in the book of 1 Samuel that God had rejected the reigning king, Saul, because of his disobedience. So he instructed the prophet Samuel to go to Bethlehem to anoint one of Jesse's sons to be the next king. David was that son.

When Samuel anointed him as king, David was a "youth" (1 Samuel 16:13. See 1 Samuel 17:33. The Hebrew word can mean an adolescent or a young man). Unfortunately for David, Samuel failed to mention—or had no idea himself—that Saul would remain on the throne for another ten years! David didn't become king over all Israel until age 30 (2 Samuel 5:4).

Between these two events, after enjoying a short period in King Saul's good graces, David's life was turned upside down with very little good happening.

Saul became obsessed with killing David. So he had his army searching high and low for him, combing the countryside. Constantly.

Saul rightly perceived David as a threat to his throne. So his life's mission became eliminating the threat. He declared David an outlaw and an enemy of the state. Anyone who aided him was guilty of treason. So David spent ten years living in the wilderness, hiding here and there, never in one place for long.

Quite a life for a king! Samuel had anointed him "king". But for ten years all he had was the name. So he waited and waited. Saul was still on the throne, and as such he was still God's anointed. And this anointed of God was constantly trying to murder David.

David must have struggled with doubt during this time. He must have wondered if Samuel had been mistaken. Or if he had misunderstood what happened that day in Bethlehem. He must have wondered if God had changed his mind, had withdrawn from him and no longer considered him a king at all. After all, God's anointed was trying to kill him. Perhaps he had God's blessing to do so.

The one constant in David's life was that he was hated and hunted, homeless and harassed for ten years. All during this time he waited for God to fulfill what he had promised years before in Bethlehem. He knew that Saul had to die for that to happen, which only God could do. So he waited, week after week, month after month, year after year. All the while having nothing but a promise given years before. All the while living in caves and just trying to survive.

Many of David's best known psalms were written during this time. They show him praying for protection, struggling to wait, and crying out to God for help. They show him going through everything from near despair to certain hope.

Eventually Saul and his sons were killed in battle, and David finally became king over all Israel. What he expresses in the opening verses of Psalm 40 reflects how he must have felt when that day finally arrived. "I waited patiently for the LORD; he inclined to me and heard my cry. He drew me up from the pit of destruction, out of the miry bog, and set my feet upon a rock, making my steps secure" (Psalm 40:1-2).

The story of David is yet another Biblical example of the strange way that God often goes about fulfilling his promises to his saints. Very slowly—from our perspective—and often allowing our lives to worsen or permitting the very opposite of what he promised to happen.

So David was writing from experience and authority when he penned the words, "Wait for the LORD. Be strong and courageous.

Wait for the LORD!" We would do well to listen!

Joseph the Dreamer

As we learned in Chapter 4, the story of Joseph, the son of Jacob and Rachel, is one of the most dramatically moving accounts in the entire Bible. It's also an outstanding example of the way God sometimes fulfills his promises.

A good student of the Bible might object, "I don't remember that God made a promise specifically to Joseph." It is true that the promise that God had made to Abraham, Isaac and Jacob, that they would have a multitude of descendants, did not pass automatically to Joseph. He was Jacob's son, yes, but so were 11 others.

But God did make a very specific promise just to Joseph. He did it through two dreams that Joseph had when he was just 17 years old.

> Now Joseph had a dream, and when he told it to his brothers they hated him even more. [6] He said to them, "Hear this dream that I have dreamed: [7] Behold, we were binding sheaves in the field, and behold, my sheaf arose and stood upright. And behold, your sheaves gathered around it and bowed down to my sheaf." [8] His brothers said to him, "Are you indeed to reign over us? Or are you indeed to rule over us?" So they hated him even more for his dreams and for his words. [9] Then he dreamed another dream and told it to his brothers and said, "Behold, I have dreamed another dream. Behold, the sun, the moon, and eleven stars were bowing down to me." [10] But when he told it to his father and to his brothers, his father rebuked him and said to him, "What is this dream that you have dreamed? Shall I and your mother and your brothers indeed come to bow ourselves to the ground before you?" [11] And his brothers were jealous of him, but his father kept the saying in mind (Genesis 37:5-11).

Some might object, "The passage quoted doesn't show any promises. It shows dreams." Actually, the quoted passage shows both.

You see, throughout the Old Testament period God used dreams to make promises and predictions. He had done so with Abraham (Genesis 15:12-21) and also Jacob (Genesis 28:10-17).

Dreams were understood to be a common way that God communicated with his prophets, as can be seen by something God said about Moses centuries later:

Hear my words: If there is a prophet among you, I the LORD make myself known to him in a vision; I speak with him in a dream. [7] Not so with my servant Moses. He is faithful in all my house. [8] With him I speak mouth to mouth, clearly, and not in riddles, and he beholds the form of the LORD' (Numbers 12:6-8).

Getting back to Joseph, Genesis also tells us that he had a unique gift for interpreting dreams. As we've already seen, years later, after he had been thrown into Pharaoh's prison, two of his fellow prisoners—Pharaoh's cupbearer and baker—had dreams, which Joseph accurately interpreted.

So two years later, when Pharaoh himself had two dreams of his own, Joseph was called from prison to interpret the dreams. After he had heard the dreams, he immediately interpreted them. Both dreams were predicting the same future reality. In Joseph's own words:

It is as I told Pharaoh; God has shown to Pharaoh what he is about to do. [29] There will come seven years of great plenty throughout all the land of Egypt, [30] but after them there will arise seven years of famine, and all the plenty will be forgotten in the land of Egypt. The famine will consume the land, [31] and the plenty will be unknown in the land by reason of the famine that will follow, for it will be very severe. [32] And the doubling of Pharaoh's dream means that the thing is fixed by God, and God will shortly bring it about (Genesis 41:28-32).

The first and last verses are crucial. Joseph told Pharaoh that through the dreams "God has shown to Pharaoh what he is about to do." In other words, the dreams were predictions or promises telling what was going to happen.

Then, in the last verse, Joseph declared that when dreams were doubled, as they were for Pharaoh, this indicated that the thing predicted in the dreams was "fixed by God" and that God would shortly bring it to pass.

Who else had had his dreams doubled years before? Joseph, of course. Therefore it is all but certain that Joseph had concluded at that time that because his own dreams had been doubled, the thing was fixed by God. Joseph believed that God was predicting/promising that he would truly reign over his family one day and they would all bow before him. The very thing that later happened when Pharaoh elevated Joseph to rule over all Egypt.

There is also every reason to believe that Joseph thought that what his dreams predicted was going to happen very soon. Why? Because, as he had said to Pharaoh, the doubling of dreams meant that God was going to bring it about *quickly*. Unfortunately, if that was his belief, he was in for a rude awakening. Because he was about to experience the lowest time of his life.

The Bottom Drops Out

As Genesis tells us, very soon after Joseph had his dreams, jealousy drove his brothers to do him great harm. They wanted to kill him, and his brother Rueben barely talked them out of it. Instead they sold him for twenty shekels of silver to a group of Midianite slave-traders who were on their way to Egypt. Then they lied to their father and led him to believe that Joseph had been killed by a wild animal.

For the next 13 years, Joseph's life went from bad to worse. The slave-traders sold him as a slave to Potiphar, Pharaoh's captain of the guard. For a time Joseph prospered in that role. But then Potiphar's wife attempted to seduce Joseph and, when he refused, she accused him of adulterous advances. Potiphar was enraged and threw him into Pharaoh's prison, which meant that he could be executed at any time.

God had promised Joseph that he would achieve greatness and would become a ruler of some kind. But instead, the exact opposite had happened. Instead of a ruler, he had become a slave.

Then, as if that hadn't been horrible enough, he was falsely accused of a crime he didn't commit. He was condemned to an undetermined time in the Pharaoh's dungeon, with no legal rights, far from his home and family. No one was there to encourage him. As far as we know, God gave him no further dreams, nor communicated with him in any way. There was nothing but silence.

He was alone. By all empirical evidence, by all outward appearances, he was utterly forgotten by God. Whatever God had seemingly promised he had apparently changed his mind. Joseph was trapped in the bottom of a pit.

He certainly knew from his father something about how God kept his promises. He knew about Abraham and Isaac. He understood that God often delayed the fulfillment of his promise. But this. This was worse.

Somehow Joseph continued to believe in God. Though he must have had horrible moments of questioning and confusion. Why was God doing this to him? Why had he promised one thing but done the opposite?

I picture Joseph asking himself, "What have I done that has so angered God that he has turned his back on me and forsaken me? It seems that he hates and despises me. I pray day and night, pleading with him to right the injustices done to me; to set me free and restore me to my father. But it doesn't happens. Nothing happens. Except more suffering. It just keeps getting worse. God is deaf to all my prayers. And it has been this way week after week, month after month and year after year."

Then there was the big letdown in prison. Joseph's hopes must have been high after he asked the cupbearer to mention him to Pharaoh, sure that at long last God was going to answer his prayers. But as we heard earlier, it wasn't to be. To have gotten his hopes up and then dashed like that, must have been crushingly disappointing.

In the End

Yet in the end God kept his promise to Joseph. And he did it in a way so breathtakingly grand that neither Joseph nor anyone else could have seen it coming.

In the space of a few hours, Joseph went from being a hopelessly condemned prisoner to Ruler over all Egypt, second only to Pharaoh in power and authority. And by his plan of storing up crops from the seven good years in order to feed people during the seven years of famine, God used Joseph to save not only the Egyptian people but people from all over the known world. Including Joseph's own father, mother and brothers. Who, by the way, did bow before him as the great lord over all Egypt.

God fulfilled his promise to Joseph. Even though it took 13 years. Even though Joseph's life went from bad to worse in the meantime. Even though the exact opposite of what God had promised happened. Even though he lost everything, including his freedom. Even though it seemed that God had changed his mind and had withdrawn his promise. Even though it seemed to Joseph that God hated him and had forsaken him. Even though it often must have seemed that there was no longer any hope.

In the end, God proved to Joseph that he is the truthful and faithful God who always keeps his promises. That he always does what he says he will do. But that the way he goes about fulfilling his promises involves confusing delays and hardships in the meantime. But eventually he works it all for good (Genesis 50:20; Romans 8:28). And even the suffering we go through in some way prepares us for the blessing to come.

The Ephesians 3:20 Factor

"Now to him who is able to do far more abundantly than all that we ask or think, according to the power at work within us" (Ephesians 3:20).

As we saw in Chapter two, at the heart of this passage is the claim that God the Father is able to do infinitely more than all we ask or think.

It also has something to say about the way God goes about fulfilling his promises.

Ephesians 3:20 tells us that God is able to do infinitely beyond all that we *think*. Infinitely beyond all the scenarios we picture to ourselves beforehand. He is able to keep his promises to us in more ways than we can possibly imagine.

Think again of Joseph. Is there really any doubt that from the moment he was sold into slavery by his brothers that he pictured to himself—imagined—how God would come to his rescue? Not only how and when the actual release would happen, but what would happen afterwards?

Do you think that Joseph ever imagined what actually did happen? Highly unlikely.

So what did happen? How did his rescue play out?

His brothers didn't immediately regret what they had done and run after the slave traders—as Joseph probably imagined they would. No one came to his rescue. He wasn't rescued sooner rather than later. Potiphar's wife didn't tell her husband the truth so that he could return to his former position.

None of the scenarios that Joseph likely imagined happened. Instead, his life kept getting worse. You know the story. You just read it!

I also think that when Joseph had pictured in his mind beforehand how God was going to answer his prayers, the *most* he imagined was freedom. That he would be set free from prison. That he would be liberated from slavery. That he would be free to return home.

But as he joyously discovered, God's method of keeping his promise towered above Joseph's imaginings. Never in his wildest dreams did Joseph imagine the way God chose.

God gave Joseph freedom *and then some*.

The same God is our God. He carries out his amazing governance now the same way he did then. He fulfills his promises in ways that are infinitely beyond all the little narrowly preconceived ways that we picture to ourselves beforehand.

So we need to remember Ephesians 3:20 when we are waiting for God to fulfill some promise to us, and it just isn't playing out the way we thought it would.

Don't be so quick to conclude that God has refused you . . . or broken his promise . . . or something worse. Don't be so quick to give up on God, or think he has given up on you.

As in the case of Joseph, in the end God gives us what we asked, and then some.

CHAPTER SIX – WHY DOES GOD KEEP HIS PROMISES THE WAY HE DOES?

If you're like me, you want to know why.

You want to know why God keeps his promises the way he does. Why so slowly? Why so painfully?

I've given this a lot of thought. Trust me.

I'm happy to report that—even though none of us can ever claim to be offering the definitive word on the subject—there are answers. There are reasons why God goes about fulfilling his promises the way he does. Good reasons. That God himself has revealed in the Scriptures.

In this chapter we will be looking at some of those reasons, in no particular order. First, though, we'll begin with something that is definitely *not* the reason.

It is Not Because God is Cruel or Has it in for You

I am supposedly a theologian, someone who has training, experience and skill in interpreting and teaching God's Word. Then why do I so easily make one of most amateurish mistakes someone can make about God?

I'm talking about the mistake of basing what God thinks of you on whatever is happening in your life at the moment. Concluding that God is favorably disposed toward you when things are going well. And concluding that he isn't when things are going bad.

So when God's provision, rescue, or whatever, hasn't materialized as promised, and life has taken an ugly turn, it is tempting—in the truest sense of the word—to conclude that he is angry at you. That he's given up on you. That's he's withdrawn his promise. Or something equally bad.

This is a deeply engrained thinking that you can see in almost all religions going back to the earliest records we have of religion. "The rivers have flooded. The crops are bad. The gods must be unhappy with us." That kind of thing.

Whatever the merit of such thinking in other religions, for those of us whose God is the God that revealed himself in Jesus Christ, it is just dumb. It is also harmful.

Listen. You can't determine what God thinks of you on the basis of the circumstances of your life. You can't because, far more often than not, "Bad things are happening," doesn't mean that the deity is smiting you.

God allows suffering in our lives for many *good* reasons. As we will see in this chapter, suffering is often a sign that God is up to something good in your life. Proof of his favor, not his disfavor.

In the same way, just because life is good doesn't mean that God is pleased with you. In the words of Jesus, God "makes his sun rise on the evil and the good, and sends rain on the just and the unjust" (Matthew 5:45).

The only reliable basis for determining what God thinks of you is the promise he's given in the gospel. Through water and the Spirit (baptism) you have been born anew into God's family as his child (John 3:5). For those who believe in Jesus Christ and have been baptized in his name, God now only sees you as a new creation in Christ (2 Corinthians 5). Your sins are covered by Christ's righteousness. You are as beloved to God as his Son is to him.

I'll add the corollary that just as you can't accurately judge what God thinks of you on the basis of your circumstances, neither can you on the basis of your *feelings*. Our feelings are usually not a reliable gauge for measuring reality. Just because you feel that God has forsaken and forgotten you, for example, doesn't at all mean he has.

Of course, many people never even consider that God might be against them, or might have forsaken of forgotten them. But some of the greatest saints have struggled with feelings of forsakenness.

Like David, who often felt forgotten and wrote about it in the psalms (Psalm 13:1, for example). He is the one who penned the famous words, "My God, my God why have you forsaken me?" (Psalm 22:1) which Jesus himself spoke on the cross.

I'm not a great saint. But I certainly have struggled with those feelings. Perhaps you have too.

A beautiful saying of Jesus comes to mind here: "Are not five sparrows sold for two pennies? And not one of them is forgotten before God. [7] Why, even the hairs of your head are all numbered. Fear not; you are of more value than many sparrows" (Luke 12:6-7).

What does this mean? First, it means that if God doesn't forget insignificant and inexpensive little sparrows, but is attentive to all their needs, neither will he forget or neglect you. Second, it means that what people think is worthless actually has great worth in God's eyes.

Third, Jesus is telling you that you have God's complete attention. He not only remembers that you exist. His eyes are constantly upon you. He sees every detail of your existence, every nook and cranny of your life, be it mind or body, be it spiritual or emotional. His attention is microscopic and profound. That is the point of Jesus declaring that God knows exactly how many hairs are on your head.

I learned long ago that people are startlingly inattentive—myself included, I'm ashamed to say. You can have a 15 minute conversation with someone without them ever noticing things about you that are obvious to you. Things that are glaring even. (Which is actually a good thing to remember when you're feeling self-conscience about something. Chances are extremely high that no one will notice!)"

Paying attention matters because I think we all know that attention and love go together. We pay attention to what we love. We pay attention to what is important to us.

Think of the person that you believe loves you more than any other. Do even they notice everything about you? Do they notice if you've gotten a haircut? Or look tired? Or don't feel well? Or are sad? Or worried? Do they notice your new shoes? Do they notice if you are wearing a different cologne or perfume, or have lost weight? Do they notice when you have a rash on your arm or a blemish on your face?

Your Father in heaven notices all of these things and far more, Jesus is telling us. He sees it all and cares about it all. Always. When things are good, and when things are bad.

God is Moving the Pieces Into Place

The first reason I want you to consider is this. God sometimes makes us wait so long because he is moving the pieces into place. It may seem like he's doing nothing. But the entire time he is working behind the scenes to get everything ready. So that he can fulfill his promise to you.

Depending on what promise you're waiting for, or what you asked, the process may be complex. Involving many people. Who must take specific actions at specific times, be in the right places at the right moments, or have just the right experiences to trigger the right ideas. Remember that these people have their own lives. Their own schedules. Their own needs. God is likely moving the pieces into place for them as well.

It's complicated. So it takes time.

Another thought. I've long observed that God almost never changes a person's character quickly. He chooses to do it slowly.

It's almost as if God knows that real character change only happens in the school of experience. So he works in the background orchestrating and engineering the right experiences. Over time. So if what we've asked God requires someone changing, it is going to take time.

You're Not Ready Yet

I enjoy eating and writing at Panera Bread. I also like to people watch there. When customers walk in and begin to look at the menu boards on the wall, you can tell by their glazed over eyes that they're overwhelmed by the choices. So the employees have been instructed to say, "Welcome to Panera. I'll help you when you're ready."

Sometimes God makes us wait and allows us to have difficulties because we're not ready to receive the blessing he means to give us. He knows that our character needs to be hammered into shape on the anvil of adversity. Only then can what he promised us fully happen.

Why did God allow Joseph to go through all that he did? Why did he permit the thirteen years of humiliation, servitude, and imprisonment so far from home? I'm convinced that God knew that Joseph wasn't ready—and never would have been ready if he had stayed at home with his family. God had to hammer his character into shape. The thirteen years of servitude and imprisonment accomplished that. Those years got Joseph in shape for the great work God had in store for him.

Sure, God could immediately give us what we ask to satisfy our immediate need or desire. But he frequently delays it, and allows us to suffer, because we're not ready. He has to hammer our characters into shape so that he can use us in greater ways—and still give us what we asked—just like Joseph.

Article: Hammering Our Characters into Shape

As you've seen, the biblical authors repeatedly tell us that God permits us to suffer in order to get our characters into the shape they need to be so that he can use us and bless us fully. ("Hammer our character into shape" is a metaphor I like to use to describe this).

The Bible describes this hammering process in several different ways. It's important that you be familiar with this language, and the teaching behind it.

Discipline

A common way that the Bible expresses the hammering process is through the language of discipline. In many places the Scriptures tell us that God disciplines us through adversity. But he does so because he loves us. (Hebrews 12:5-11).

- My son, do not despise the LORD's discipline or be weary of his reproof, [12] for the LORD reproves him whom he loves, as a father the son in whom he delights (Proverbs 3:11-12).
- "Behold, blessed is the one whom God reproves; therefore despise not the discipline of the Almighty (Job 5:17).
- God is treating you as sons. For what son is there whom his father does not discipline? [8] If you are left without discipline, in which all have participated, then you are illegitimate children and not sons. [9] Besides this, we have had earthly fathers who disciplined us and we respected them. Shall we not much more be subject to the Father of spirits and live? [10] For they disciplined us for a short time as it seemed best to them, but he disciplines us for our good, that we may share his holiness (Hebrews 12:7-10).
- Those whom I love, I reprove and discipline (Revelation 3:19).

One of the most despicable complaints I ever made to God was that earthly fathers are more loving than he is. I never said it in so many words, but that was the gist.

What I said was, "Most earthly fathers would do anything to help their child, but often they are powerless to do so. And it just kills them that they can't. But you, our Father in heaven, who supposedly loves us, you do have the power, you can help your children, but you do nothing and leave them in their misery. What kind of father does that?"

What a terrible thought. One that I confessed as sin when I came to my senses.

It is true that many fathers—if it is within their power to do so—will immediately deliver their children from whatever difficulty they face. And yes, it is true that by doing so these fathers demonstrate their love for their children.

But there is wise fatherly love and there is unwise fatherly love.

Unwise love always gets the child out of the mess he's in right away. But it doesn't consider what is best for the child's development in the long run.

Unwise love often is enabling. It can enable the child to never grow up. Or it can enable him to remain in some self-defeating or sinful pattern of behavior.

If a loving father were to always immediately rescue his child from trouble, then that child might never experience the negative consequences of his actions. Which could lead to his repeating the same negative behavior endlessly. It could prevent him from learning and growing and reaching maturity.

Every parent wants to make whatever pain the child is experiencing to stop. To "make it better." But struggles, problems, difficulties, obstacles and pain are often the only way that we grow or make the changes we need to make.

And problems and suffering are God's primary method of discipline. Let me repeat that for emphasis: *Problems and suffering are God's primary method of discipline*. Earthly parents have their methods of discipline. God has his. Both forms of discipline are motivated by love.

If God always immediately fulfilled his promises to us, it would hurt us eventually. We would likely be spoiled, immature, lazy and have an entitlement mentality. Our entire view of reality would be horribly skewed and disfigured. Our world would become ridiculously small, eventually containing nothing more than ourselves and our own little wants and needs.

Along the same lines, easy success is almost never a good thing in the long run. If everything we wanted or needed came too easily or quickly we would likely never learn important things about ourselves that we need to know; things that only failure or setbacks can teach us. We might never develop important character traits like resiliency, dogged persistence, and determination. We might not acquire skills essential for the vocation or life God has called us to.

Pruning

Another metaphor we see in the Bible that tells us that God uses adversity for our good is pruning. Just as a gardener prunes fruit bearing bushes and trees so they might continue to thrive and produce fruit, so does God. Jesus uses this metaphor in John 15.

- "I am the true vine, and my Father is the vinedresser. [2] Every branch in me that does not bear fruit he takes away, and every branch that does bear fruit he prunes, that it may bear more fruit (John 15:1-2).

Jesus tells his disciples that the Father doesn't prune every branch connected to the vine. He only prunes the branches (Christians) that bear fruit. He does it not to inflict pain on the branches. He does it so that the branches might thrive and bear even more fruit.

So if you are suffering, it could be a sign of God's approval, not his disapproval. It could also be a sign that God is preparing to use you in a greater way.

Testing

When the Biblical authors speak of God testing our faith, they usually aren't thinking of the testing that happens at school. The kind that your graded on. Rather, they have in mind the testing that smiths do to precious metals, like gold and silver.

When first taken out of the ground, both gold and silver have other "impure" metals mixed in, such as iron and copper. In ancient times the smith tested, or refined, the gold (or silver) by subjecting it to intense heat, after first adding lead to it. Once the gold melted down to molten liquid, the lead caused the impurities to rise to the top, forming a thin layer. The smith would then blow the impurities (also called dross) off. What was left was pure gold.

Just as smiths tested metals in the fire, so God tests believers in the fire of adversity.

- "I will turn my hand against you and will smelt away your dross as with lye and remove all your alloy. [26] And I will restore your judges as at the first, and your counselors as at the beginning. Afterward you shall be called the city of righteousness, the faithful city" (Isaiah 1:25-26).
- "The crucible is for silver, and the furnace is for gold, and the LORD tests hearts" (Proverbs 17:3).
- "Behold, I have refined you, but not as silver; I have tried you in the furnace of affliction" (Isaiah 48:10).
- "But he knows the way that I take; when he has tried me, I shall come out as gold" (Job 23:10).
- "For gold is tested in the fire, and those found acceptable, in the furnace of humiliation" (Sirach 2:5).

Just as the smith uses fire to remove impurities from gold, thereby making it pure gold, so God uses suffering to remove impurities from us, resulting in a purer and a more effective faith.

Article: God Tests Abraham

Occasionally the Scriptures do speak of God testing our faith as a kind of examination. The prototypical example is God's testing of Abraham in Genesis 22. God commanded Abraham to kill Isaac and offer him as a sacrifice.

> After these things God tested Abraham and said to him, "Abraham!" And he said, "Here am I." [2] He said, "Take your son, your only son Isaac, whom you love, and go to the land of Moriah, and offer him there as a burnt offering on one of the mountains of which I shall tell you. . . When they came to the place of which God had told him, Abraham built the altar there and laid the wood in order and bound Isaac his son and laid him on the altar, on top of the wood. [10] Then Abraham reached out his hand and took the

knife to slaughter his son. [11] But the angel of the
LORD called to him from heaven and said,
"Abraham, Abraham!" And he said, "Here am I." [12]
He said, "Do not lay your hand on the boy or do
anything to him, for now I know that you fear God,
seeing you have not withheld your son, your only
son, from me." (Genesis 22:1-2, 9-12).

Much is made of the fact that Abraham obeyed God's
command to offer up Isaac as a sacrifice to him. Much is
made of his obedience.

But was it simply a matter of blind obedience? Or was it a
matter of Abraham being so certain that God must keep his
promise, that he knew that Isaac would be fine?

God had promised Abraham that through Isaac he would
have a multitude of descendants. If Isaac died God would be
breaking his promise. In Abraham's mind that was impossible.
Therefore, either God wasn't going to make him do it ("God
will provide a sacrifice, my son" Genesis 22:7-8); or he was
going to raise Isaac from the dead if necessary (Hebrews
11:17-19). Because Abraham believed it was impossible for
God to break a promise. That promise. Any promise.

Abraham was so willing and obedient because of his faith
in God's promise. He was no glassy-eyed thrall who would
have blindly obeyed anything God said.

Abraham's faith was being tested. But the faith that was
being tested was his faith in God's promise that through Isaac
all the nations of the earth would be blessed. Not merely his
faith in God's goodness or wisdom.

In other words, this particular episode is a marvelous
example of someone being so certain that it was impossible
for God to break his promise that he was willing to risk all,
even his own son.

It also is a marvelous example of someone being so certain
that what God had promised would happen, that he is willing
to endure the opposite happening.

Of course, whoever wrote the letter to the Hebrews is all
over this. He understood that faith in the promises was at the
heart of everything that happened there.

> By faith Abraham, when he was tested, offered up
> Isaac, and he who had received the promises was in
> the act of offering up his only son, of whom it was
> said, "Through Isaac shall your offspring be named."
> He considered that God was able even to raise him
> from the dead, from which, figuratively speaking, he
> did receive him back (Hebrews 11:17-19).

So That We Won't Love the Gifts More Than the Giver

A third reason that God fulfills his promises the way he does is so we won't love the gifts more than the Giver. So that we won't love the promises fulfilled more than the one who made and kept the promises.

Martin Luther says this so well.

> This is the constant course of the church at all times, namely, that promises are made and that then those who believe the promises are treated in such a way that they are compelled to wait for things that are invisible, to believe what they do not see, and to hope for what does not appear. He who does not do this is not a Christian.
>
> Moreover, God does this in order to test our hearts, whether we are willing to do without the promised blessings for a time. We shall not do without them forever. This is certain. And if God did not test us and postpone His promises, we would not be able to love Him wholeheartedly. For if He immediately gave everything He promises, we would not believe but would immerse ourselves in the blessings that are at hand and forget God (Martin Luther, "Lectures on Genesis: Chapters 26-30," AE 5:202).

Isn't it well known that parents who immediately indulge their child's every whim are eventually neither respected nor loved? They are seen as a means to an end. As bank tellers. Cash dispensers. Genies.

The very same thing can, and does happen with God's children.

It's Not About You Right Now

Sometimes the reason God is making you wait for the promised thing to happen is because it isn't about you right now.

For example, let's say you're a recent college graduate living with your parents. You've been waiting for God to give you direction, as he's promised. Or to provide you with a job. Or to let you live on your own.

But nothing happens. You desperately want to move forward with your life, but you can't. You feel trapped. Frozen in place. Your life is going nowhere.

It could be that God is saying to you, "What I have promised will happen. What you are waiting for will come. But right now, it isn't about you. Right now it is about your parents. They need you there with them."

If you've been waiting for God to answer your prayer for something of importance in your life, and nothing has happened, then consider this reason as a possibility. Perhaps God temporarily has you where you are for the benefit of someone else. Right now it isn't about you. It's about them.

Another Way Will Give God More Glory

Another reason God may be making you wait is because he is lining up a particular time and place that will bring him more glory. By "glory" I mean "credit" or "praise."

I believe that the more obvious it is that God did it—that he answered your prayer or kept another kind of promise—the more glory he receives. A very clear example of this occurs in the story of Gideon in the book of Judges, chapters 6 and 7.

God called Gideon to deliver his people from the oppression of Midian, a neighboring nation that had invaded Israel some 7 years earlier. So oppressive was their rule that many Israelites fled into the hills and lived in caves. Their army was enormous, far outnumbering anything that Israel could muster.

After God called him, Gideon sent out messengers to several of the twelve tribes of Israel calling upon every abled-bodied man to take part in overthrowing the Midianites. Some 32,000 men responded and came to Gideon at Mt. Gilead.

When God saw how many had gathered, he made this unusual comment to Gideon: "The people with you are too many for me to give the Midianites into their hand, lest Israel boast over me, saying, 'My own hand has saved me.'" (Judges 7:2). So he instructed Gideon to tell the men that anyone who was afraid should leave—and 22,000 turned tail and departed, leaving 10,000.

God wasn't satisfied. He told Gideon there were still too many. He gave further instructions. In the end, only 300 soldiers remained. God was satisfied: "With the 300 I will save you and deliver the Midianites into your hand" (Judges 7:7). Which is precisely what happened.

Though it certainly isn't always the case, the account of Gideon shows us that God sometimes desires to work in such a way that it is obvious that he—and he alone—was the one who did it. Because it brings him greater glory.

God could easily give you what you've asked when and how you want it. But perhaps if he did, he wouldn't receive as much glory. Because it wouldn't be nearly as obvious that "God did it."

Perhaps He Wants to Return us to our Created State

There is something very important to recognize that must be kept in mind when considering how and when God keeps his promises. It is this. We were created to depend on God for all things. It is part of our design specification. Being dependent on God is the shape God wants to hammer us into.

There will be times in the lives of some Christians' lives when God, out of love, will humble them and reduce them to nearly nothing. In order to teach them again to depend on him—and not themselves—for all things.

Especially will this be the case if he sees that they are becoming dangerously self-sufficient. Self-sufficiency when taken to its extreme is a great enemy to Christian faith. For it often is a precursor to falling away from God.

For example, when we are financially secure, with money put away for all exigencies, it is very easy to forget God. Because we never need him. It is also very easy to think that whatever prosperity we have achieved is the result of our own efforts—thus becoming our own gods. If we die in this condition we lose our souls. "What does it profit a man to gain the whole world, yet forfeit his soul" (Mark 8:36)?

Why did Jesus teach us to pray "give us this day our *daily* bread?" So that we would depend on God each day for everything.

Why did God give manna one day at a time to the Israelites in the wilderness? Why did this manna spoil so quickly that it was impossible to put any aside for future needs? So that they would depend on God daily for all that they needed.

Why, when the people were ready to enter the Promised Land, did Moses warn them not to forget God in prosperity (Deuteronomy 8)? Because it is so easy to do and the consequences to us are so harmful.

Sometimes the reason that God delays fulfilling his promises to us, or even permits the opposite to happen, is because we have begun to think that we are the "architects of our own reality." Which is just another way of saying that we are own gods. To die in this condition is to lose all. So he permits us to go through times of want to teach us this again, and to force us to see clearly that we were created to depend on him.

Article: That We Might Not Rely on Ourselves but on God

> For we do not want you to be ignorant, brothers, of the affliction we experienced in Asia. For we were so utterly burdened beyond our strength that we despaired of life itself. [9] Indeed, we felt that we had received the sentence of death. But that was to make us rely not on ourselves but on God who raises the dead (2 Corinthians 1:8-9).

In his second letter to the Christians at Corinth, Paul tells them about a particular affliction that he and his coworkers experienced in the province of Asia. It was so terrible an affliction that they were "so utterly burdened beyond our strength that we despaired of life itself." They believed they were at death's door.

Paul tells them that the purpose of it all, "was to make us rely not on ourselves but on God who raises the dead."

This is a marvelous statement that can only be fully understood by those who have also been "so utterly burdened beyond their strength that they despair of life." Who truly believe that their lives are over and that there is no longer any hope. To the question, "Why does God allow us to suffer so?" Paul offers the answer, "To make us rely not on ourselves but on God who raises the dead."

Of course his answer begs another question: "Why is it important that we rely/depend on God and not on ourselves?" Especially when in Western culture over the last 300 years the exact opposite has been taught.

In the current culture, to be dependent on anyone or anything other than yourself is a major sign of weakness—perhaps even sickness. Even two people who are highly dependent on each other are deemed to be "sick" according to psychology. They are "codependents." We are told that a superior person is *independent*.

Similarly, to wait for God to rescue you is ridiculed. To be passive is excoriated as the height of weakness or stupidity. Thus says the world.

The Christian religion says that God wants us to depend on him rather than on ourselves. That sometimes he permits us to be so overwhelmed by adversity that our own strength, resources, resolve, and resiliency fails us, and we have no recourse left but to rely on God rather than ourselves.

Why does God want it this way? First, we were made to be that way. We were created to be dependent on God. We are healthiest and happiest when we do. It is our normal or default orientation.

Second, he is glorified when we depend on him for all that we want or need. What glory does he receive if we depend on ourselves only? If we overcome our problems and difficulties through our own strength and wits?

Third, because every single human being really is dependent on God for all things, whether they realize it or not.

Fourth, because we need to be reminded that "The LORD, he is God." We aren't.

The God who has revealed himself through the prophets and the apostles, who became incarnate in the person of Jesus Christ, not only created us, and not only saved us from eternal death, but he also lives to save us from all our troubles. He was and always is our Savior.

If even the great apostle Paul needed to be "reminded" to depend on God and not on himself and his coworkers, than that is a powerful indication that all Christians do.

Teaching itself is not enough. We can know and believe the Biblical teaching that we should depend on God and not on ourselves or someone else and yet still "kick against the goads." Yet still fight the whole notion of having to depend on God.

Because of our residual fallenness, we chafe at being a dependent on anyone, human or divine.

Who knew better than Paul that he could do nothing apart from Jesus Christ? He's the one that wrote, "By the grace of God I am what I am;" "I can do all things through him who strengthens me;" "Our sufficiency is not in ourselves;" "I worked harder than the rest but it was not I but the grace of God in me."

Nevertheless, because of his sinful nature, a stronger instruction was needed. The instruction of severe adversity.

In the very same way many of us who already know that we should depend on God and not on ourselves may also need to be schooled in severe adversity to truly learn it.

As to Paul, was that not what was going on with his thorn in the flesh? The thorn hampered him in some way. Christ's words to him are couched in words of dependence: "My grace is sufficient for you. For my power is made perfect in weakness." Which means, "You're still depending on yourself, Paul. You think the success of your work depends on your strength, your health and your person. It doesn't. You should only depend on me. My grace is sufficient for you, etc."

Human beings were created to be dependents of God. Their whole life through. From birth to death.

The movement to Christian maturity is not a movement from dependence to independence as is the case with the movement to physical and emotional maturity.

So if the bottom has dropped out of your life . . . or if you have lost everything . . . or if you have utterly failed . . . or if you are facing a crisis that overwhelms your ability to cope . . . then you are *blessed*.

God is "reminding" you that you are meant to be his dependent. He is about to do something great in your life. And when you are delivered and rescued and restored and renewed, it will be obvious that the living God did it.

When your strength has failed you. When you have been stretched beyond your limit. When you are at your wits end. When your hope is gone. When you feel that you've died or want to. When there seems no way out or no way forward. When all doors seemed closed and locked and none are open. When all options have been exhausted and no possibilities remain. Then, trust in your God. Rely on him. Depend on his strength, his power, his infinite resources, his wisdom, his love, his grace and his promises to help you no matter how impossible your circumstances seem.

What seems impossible to you is eminently possible to him. What is hopeless to you is the height of simplicity to him.

He can and will raise you up again. He can and will save you.
Just stand still and you will see the deliverance of the LORD.

So that You Have Interactions

Life is about interactions. The interactions we have with people. Each day brings them. Each one is a God-given opportunity to be used by God to his glory. To be lights in the world (Matthew 5:14-16). Even if we do nothing more than pray for the people we meet in these interactions, then the person we've interacted with will be blessed and God will be glorified.

God may be postponing the fulfillment of his promises to you so that you have interactions. Interactions that you otherwise would not have had. Interactions that he wants you to have. Interactions that for some reason are important for you to have.

A person may not be healed immediately, for example, so that they see another doctor and have interactions they otherwise wouldn't have had.

Remember that we have been placed on this earth to be a blessing to as many people as possible.

The Nature of our Request Requires it: James and John's Request (Mark 10:35-45)

Sometimes the reason God makes us wait so long and suffer in the meantime is because our particular request requires it. The account of James and Johns' prayer illustrates this powerfully.

Mark records that the brothers James and John came to Jesus and said, "Teacher, we want you to do for us whatever we ask of you." Jesus replied, "What do you want me to do for you?" They said, "Grant us to sit, one on your right hand and on your left, in your glory."

Jesus said, "You do not know what you are asking. Are you able to drink the cup that I will drink? And to be baptized with the baptism in which I will be baptized?" They said, "We are able." The Lord replied, "You will drink the cup that I will drink and be baptized in the baptism that I will. But to sit at my right and left is not mine to grant, but it is for those for whom it has been prepared."

This is such an important text on the topic of prayer. This is such a crucial text on the topic of how God keeps his promises.

But so much attention has been paid to other elements of this account that this highly significant teaching on the way God answers prayers has been missed.

When we examine the passage, we see that, first, the brothers demonstrate that they had heard and understood Jesus' promises of prayer correctly. The phrasing of their request sounds almost exactly like the various "whatever" promises of Jesus, as recorded, for example in Mark 11, John 14, and John 16. "We want you to do for us whatever we ask of you." Just as Jesus had promised them he would do.

Second, notice that Jesus did not scold or rebuke them. He didn't say to them, "Where did you ever get the silly idea that I would give you *whatever you asked*? What a childish notion!" Or "I know I said "whatever" but come on! Seriously?"

Third, note that Jesus didn't say, "No" at first. The first thing he said after hearing their request was, "You don't know what you are asking." Then he asked them if they were able to drink the same cup and be baptized with the same baptism that Jesus himself would. Drinking the cup and being baptized were figures of speech for his suffering and death.

I can almost see the love in Jesus' eyes as he explained it to James and John. "You don't know what you are asking. You don't realize what will need to happen for your request to be granted. For your prayer to be granted it will be necessary for you to suffer martyrdom as I will. You will have to go through much suffering before that request is granted."

I think that God responds similarly to some of our requests. We, like James and John, take him up on his "whatever" promises of prayer. We ask him to give us what we want. And he says, "You don't know what you're asking." Except, unlike Christ's final answer to James and John, God often says "Yes" to our requests.

He says to us, "Okay. I will give you that. Even though you don't realize all you will have to experience before it is given you. You don't know all that has to happen first. It is going to take far longer than you think. The very opposite of what you ask will happen along the way. You will have to suffer so that I can hammer you into the shape you need to be in to receive it. You will have to greatly persevere. It will be a hard test of faith. But in the end I will give you what you ask."

I believe that many of our requests require us to "drink cups" and to "be baptized with baptisms" before the requests can be granted. But not understanding this, we wrongly interpret all that happens along the way as God emphatically saying, "No!" And so we then take matters into our own hands so as to get in another way what we asked God. Or we just give up. By so doing we lose the blessing.

In Conclusion . . .

What I set out to do in this chapter is to give you a taste of some of the good reasons God has for keeping his promises the way he sometimes does. Making us wait. Permitting suffering. Making it seem that he isn't going to keep them at all.

But what I've written here is just a taste. Only a taste of the infinite number of good reasons that God has for doing it this way.

He does know what he's doing. He does have your very best interest in mind. What he promised is most certainly going to happen. And the way he has chosen to do it—though it may seem arbitrarily cruel to you right now—will prove to be the wisest course possible. You'll see.

CHAPTER SEVEN – WHY IT MATTERS

So now you know that God has a method that he uses in keeping his promises. But does it really matter that you know it?

It does matter. A lot. Not knowing how God goes about keeping his promises can lead to all kinds of negative faith complications. In this chapter we will look at some of these potential complications.

Why Only Two of the Adults Who Left Egypt Entered the Promised Land

"And now I am about to go the way of all the earth, and you know in your hearts and souls, all of you, that not one word has failed of all the good things that the LORD your God promised concerning you. All have come to pass for you; not one of them has failed" (Joshua 23:14)

Joshua spoke these words to the second generation of Israelites that had made the exodus out of Egypt. Joshua spoke these words to the *second* generation because the first generation had all died.

This is a crucial fact. Why? Because it tells us something of great importance about how God keeps his promises—and why it matters whether we know it or not.

Through Moses, God had also made the same promise to that first generation, those who were adults when the exodus from Egypt occurred. It was his intention to fulfill this promise for that first generation. It was his intention to bring that first generation into the Promised Land and give it to them.

But because of their repeated failure to believe the promise, they didn't make it. God made them wander in the wilderness for 40 years until they all died. Of all those first generation adults, only Caleb and

Joshua entered the Promised Land.

God made a promise to all his people. Yet only two of those who were adults at the time entered the land of promise. Only two experienced the fulfillment of the promise.

What happened? Did God break his promise? Did he fail to do what he had promised? Joshua, in the above passage, says, "No." "All the good things that the LORD your God promised concerning you came to pass."

Yet there is no escaping the fact that, except for Joshua and Caleb, not a single one of the hundreds of thousands of adults experienced the fulfillment of the promise. They made it to the very border of the Promised Land—but failed to enter it.

What doomed them, essentially, was that *they stumbled over the way in which God was keeping his promise.*

When they left Egypt were they expecting to go straight to the Promised Land? With no mishaps along the way? We can't know. What we do know is that they didn't go straight to the Promised Land, and they did have many mishaps along the way.

God chose to fulfill the promise of the land slowly. With adversity. And with a dizzying array of unexpected changes.

From the moment they departed Egypt, they encountered hardships they probably hadn't expected, each one challenging their belief that God would indeed keep his promise.

They had to give up all the previous creature comforts in Egypt and live out in the middle of a forbidding desert for over two years. In Egypt they were slaves. The Egyptians nearly worked them to death. But at least they had their own houses. At least they had plenty of food and drink.

Now they were living out in the wilds, exposed to the elements. They ran out of food. They experienced hunger and the fear of starvation. More than once they had no water. Nothing in their life experience had prepared them for any of this. And this kind of thing went on and on.

The Amalekites came out to wage war against them. Israel won, but certainly many husbands and sons were killed or wounded. These men weren't soldiers. They had never in their lives fought in a battle.

They were challenged by Moses "disappearance" for 40 days and 40 nights after he ascended Mt. Sinai. They were told that he had gone up to meet with God at the summit. But no one told them—because no one knew beforehand—how long it would take. Forty days and nights is a long time. When Moses failed to return, they were filled with doubts. Was he ever coming back? Was he even alive?

Everything they had known changed. God established an entirely new life for them. A highly structured life. A life with many new commandments. Many new laws. Many new rituals, ceremonies and holy days. They hadn't anticipated any of these changes, I'm sure. How could they have?

Finally, they arrived at the border of the Promised Land. But before they entered they sent twelve spies into the land to do reconnaissance and then report back.

When the spies returned, they told the people about the bounty of the land. But, unfortunately, ten of the twelve spies terrified them with their report of the people who already lived there. They told them that the people were mighty warriors living in heavily fortified cities. Some of them were giants. To enter this land would be certain death for them and their children, they claimed.

This last test of the people's faith in God's promise pushed them over the edge. The almost couldn't believe what they heard. But— unfortunately for them—they did believe it. They were terrified and angry.

After all they had endured in the wilderness for nearly two years, now this? They finally arrived at the border of the promised land, only to learn that the entire journey had been for nothing. They decided to choose a new leader and return to Egypt. They were about to stone Moses and Aaron, and would have, if hadn't God intervened.

Not only had they not anticipated that it would take so long to get to the land of promise. Not only had they not planned on all the hardships and all the changes. It seems that they hadn't expected fortified cities populated with intimidating people. Apparently they expected the land would be empty and ready for immediate occupancy. It wasn't. So they gave up on God's promise altogether.

God had had enough. There were limits even to his divine patience. The people complained one too many times about the way he was choosing to fulfill his promise. Now they had given up on the promise completely. They chose to believe the terrifying word of the spies—and rejected the hopeful word of God's promise.

So God swore that none of the people 20 years of age and older would enter the Promised Land. They would die in the wilderness. Their children would enter, but only after wandering in the wilderness for 40 years.

The point I'm *not* making is that God will punish anyone who gives up on his promises. Or doubts them one too many times.

The point of my telling this tragic affair is that it is a powerful illustration of how God goes about fulfilling his promises. That he doesn't always fulfill his promises in the way that we hope or expect. Not when we think he will, nor how we think he will. The fulfillment will frequently come neither immediately or smoothly.

As we wait for the fulfillment, things that we never anticipated may happen to us, too. As with the Israelites who left Egypt, we may have to pass through hardships that test our faith to its very limits. Lifeless "deserts." Periods of silence and confusion. Frightening "giants" and "fortified cities". Counterintuitive setbacks and suffering. All of which will make the fulfilling of God's promise seem impossible, on the one hand, or utter deception on the other.

If this happens, therefore, or when it happens, we should not be surprised or bewildered. For all of it is the anvil upon which God is hammering our character into the shape it needs to be in. All of it is happening for good reasons. Reasons that are good for us. As we have seen.

If this happens, we should realize that the forces of darkness will try to use it to "sift us like wheat" and cast us into utter unbelief, as they did the Israelites, so that we lose out on the fulfillment of the promises.

If this happens, we should realize that such is the way that God goes about the business of keeping his promises; and—no matter how strange and troubling it may seem to us—we should realize that all is well.

And no matter what, we must not stop believing that God will keep his promise to us. We must remain certain that he will. We must not give up.

Whenever we find ourselves questioning whether God will keep his promises . . . whenever we find ourselves questioning God's character (if God was truly faithful, loving and gracious, he would have kept his promise by now and would not have allowed me to suffer in this way) . . . or whenever we find ourselves questioning God's existence (is any of this even real?), then we should immediately repent of our doubt and disbelief, and ask God to restore our faith. And we should recall that God is fulfilling his promises in the way that he always has.

If we persevere in faith, and continue to believe that God will fulfill all that he has promised, we will discover in the end that he will. We will joyfully receive the benefits of the promise. We will enter "the Promised Land."

Prematurely Concluding that God has said "No"

One of the most common negative consequences of not knowing how God sometimes goes about fulfilling his promises is that we prematurely conclude that God has said no and then "move on."

Isn't this what we all do? If we ask God for something and "too much" time passes without receiving what we asked, we assume that he has said no. Or if the opposite seems to happen, don't we immediately conclude that God has said no? Once we make that premature assumption, we give up on the prayer and move on.

When we do this we risk missing out completely on the answer to our prayer. How so? By "taking matters into our own hands," perhaps. Or by "settling." Or by giving up on what we wanted and moving on to something completely different in a way that hinders God from helping us.

For example, perhaps God was going to answer our prayer to lead us to just the right mate. But when too much time passed we became impatient, even desperate. And we rushed into a relationship that was bad for us. Or married someone ill-suited for us.

Not Understanding Can Seriously Undermine our Faith Without Us Ever Noticing

Not knowing something about the way God fulfills his promises can also seriously undermine our faith.

Here is a simple example. A Christian reads the words of Jesus in Matthew 7:7, "Ask and it will be given you. Seek and you will find. Knock and the door will be opened to you." Buoyed by that promise of prayer, he cries out to God, asking him to grant something he truly needs.

But nothing happens. So the Christian continues to plead with God, reminding him of his promise. Still nothing happens. Weeks pass. Or perhaps many months go by.

The Christian anguishes over this, wondering what is wrong. Wondering why God is refusing his prayer. Wondering how what he asked could possibly not be God's will. Then the same thing happens with a different promise and a different prayer.

Disappointed and disillusioned, the Christian finally stops praying, concluding that God has obviously said no. Or that God is displeased with him in some way. Or that prayer doesn't work. Or that the Bible can't be trusted. Or that God doesn't exist. His faith in God is undermined, weakened, or even lost.

Had he known that God frequently keeps his promises slowly and makes us wait, would he have gone through the same emotional turmoil? Would he have so easily concluded that God had said no and stopped praying? Would he have given up and potentially lost out on God's blessing? Would his trust in God have been undermined?

Very likely, none of these faith complications would have happened had he known something about the way God goes about keeping his promises.

I have the sense that the grim picture I've painted in my example has actually happened to an untold number of Christians. Perhaps you're one of them.

Christians whose faith has been undermined or lost because they didn't understand God's method of promise-keeping. Not understanding, they came to all kinds of false and unfortunate conclusions about God, about the Biblical promises, and about prayer. They reached the conclusion that regardless of what the Bible says about these things, the reality is something else altogether.

But there's something else just as tragic that can happen. Having been frequently disappointed by God seemingly not answering their prayers, many Christians unconsciously *adjust* by downgrading their expectations. So that they no longer expect God to give them what they ask. In fact they expect him not to.

They conclude, for whatever reason, that nothing they ask is right in God's sight. So they stop asking. Or, they continue to ask, but their requests really ask nothing. Becoming little more than "Thy will be done" and "Be with so and so." They no longer expect God to actually respond to their pleas for help. They eventually come to expect nothing of God at all.

Almost imperceptibly, their Christianity becomes nothing more than a remembrance of what God did long ago . . . and a looking forward to what God will do at the end of time. Rather than an expectation of what that same God has promised to do in their lives now.

Their Christianity becomes nothing more than the recalling and celebration of history and the anticipation of futurity. It becomes nothing more than the study of historical texts; the recitation of ancient stories and liturgies; the talk of heaven and the life to come. Their faith encompasses what God did and what God will do, but not what God is doing and can do now.

Their Christianity ceases to be a vibrant belief in what the living God has promised to do for them—and does do for them—in the present.

If that isn't tragic I don't know what is.

So I hope you can see that knowing something about how God keeps his promises can make an enormous difference. To say the least.

God Wants You to Test Him

God wants you to test him.

Wait. Isn't that the opposite of what the Bible says? Not really. The Bible does warn us about a certain kind of testing God that is sin.

We test God sinfully when we test his patience by refusing to trust or obey him. As we just read about the Israelites in the wilderness.

We test God sinfully when we take foolish or dangerous risks to see if God will keep his word and rescue us. This is what Satan was tempting Jesus to do when he told him to jump off the pinnacle of the temple in order to demonstrate his faith in God (Matthew 4:5-7). This is what snake handlers are doing.

We test God sinfully when we withhold faith or love for God unless he proves himself in a manner of our choosing. This is like the Pharisees and Sadducees asking Jesus to perform a sign to test him (Mark 8:11-12). Or like the atheist who tells everyone that he will believe in God if and when God appears to him.

But there is a testing of God that pleases him immensely. A testing that he not only tolerates but wants.

We test God in this God-pleasing sense when he promises to do something and we take him up on it. We test the promise to see if it is true. God wants us to test his promises to see if they are true.

We see this in Malachi 3. The Israelites had not been tithing (giving ten percent), which Old Testament believers were commanded to do. From the beginning God had promised that those who tithed would be blessed. That he would reward the tither by opening his storehouse of blessings upon them (e.g., Proverbs 3:9-10).

Through the prophet Malachi, God repeats this to the Israelites and invites them to test him to see if this promise would prove true for them.

> Bring the full tithe into the storehouse, that there may be food in my house. And thereby put me to the test, says the LORD of hosts, if I will not open the windows of heaven for you and pour down for you a blessing until there is no more need (Malachi 3:10).

God specifically says, "Put me to the test, if I will not open the windows of heaven for you and pour down for you a blessing until there is no more need." In other words, "Test this promise of mine, and see for yourself whether this promise will prove true for you or not."

We also see this in Psalm 34. In the beginning of this psalm, David praises God for delivering him from his troubles. He shares his personal experience with God.

> I sought the LORD, and he answered me and delivered me from all my fears. [5] Those who look to him are radiant, and their faces shall never be ashamed. [6] This poor man cried, and the LORD heard him and saved him out of all his troubles (Psalm 34:4-6).

Then he turns to the listener/reader of this psalm and addresses them. "Oh, taste and see that the LORD is good! Blessed is the man who takes refuge in him" (Psalm 34:8).

David invites all who hear or read this psalm to "Taste and see that the LORD is good." But what does it mean to "taste and see that the LORD is good" other than "Test God to see that the Lord is good. Don't take my word for it. Try God's promises out for yourself. Trust him like I did. Ask him to deliver you from troubles as he has promised to do, and find out for yourself whether he does."

Such a person is "blessed," David writes, because they find out for themselves that God is a God who does what he promises. They discover for themselves the love and power of God.

Peter echoes the same thought when in his first epistle he encourages his readers, "Like newborn infants, long for the pure spiritual milk, that by it you may grow up into salvation—if indeed you have tasted that the Lord is good" (1 Peter 2:2-3). Those who have already tasted that the Lord is good, who have experienced that he keeps the promises recorded in the Scriptures, will indeed long for the pure milk of the Word, to discover all of the promises he has made.

Now here is the thing. When God invites us to test him in this way and we refuse, we really make him unhappy. When God makes magnificent offers to us, promising to freely give us something, and we don't, we *weary* God. Weary God? Yes, weary God. There is an explicit example of this in the Bible.

When Ahaz was king of Judah, the kings of Israel and Syria were threatening invasion. The combined forces of these two armies would have overwhelmed Judah's resources. Understandably, Ahaz was shaken.

So God sent the prophet Isaiah to Ahaz with an amazing offer. First he promised Ahaz that the plans of these two kings would fail. Then he went even further. To bolster Ahaz's faith in the promise he had just made, God invited the king to ask for any sign of his choosing, to prove that the promise would indeed come true.

> Again the LORD spoke to Ahaz, [11] "Ask a sign of the LORD your God; let it be deep as Sheol or high as heaven." [12] But Ahaz said, "I will not ask, and I will not put the LORD to the test." [13] And he said, "Hear then, O house of David! Is it too little for you to weary men, that you weary my God also? [14] Therefore the Lord himself will give you a sign. Behold, the virgin shall conceive and bear a son, and shall call his name Immanuel" (Isaiah 7:10-14).

Unfortunately, Ahaz refused God's gracious offer. He refused to take God up on it, claiming—wrongly—that to do so would be testing God in the sinful sense. "I will not ask, and I will not put the LORD to the test." Notice that Ahaz masked his foolishness in pious language. "No, I would never do such a thing! That would be testing God. I will not ask!"

A frustrated Isaiah responds, "So it isn't enough that you weary your subjects? But you have to weary God also?!"

We weary God when he makes wonderfully gracious offers to us and we don't test these promises for ourselves to see if they are true. Especially if we think that doing so would be sin. Like King Ahaz did.

As you've seen throughout the book, God has made innumerable promises to us in the Scriptures. "Ask and it will be given you." "Call upon me in the day of trouble and I will rescue you." "Those who seek the LORD lack no good thing." He wants us to test these promises for ourselves to not only discover that he is a God who keeps his promises, but also that he might show forth his goodness in the form of blessings for us, which he absolutely loves to do.

O, taste and see that the LORD is good! To God, it isn't enough that you believe that other believers tasted and experienced God's goodness. He wants you to taste him yourself. So taste!

You Don't Have Because You Don't Ask

If you read Chapter two, then you know yourself that the Bible contains many promises of prayer. In which God promises to give us whatever we ask. He promises this not once. Not twice. But many times. In these promises he urges, exhorts and invites us to take him up on his offer.

Why is this? It is because God wants us to ask him for much so he can give us much. How many times does Jesus have to urge us to "ask" before we understand this?

The more we ask, the more God can give. The more we ask, the more blessings we receive.

But the flipside is also true. The less we ask, the less God can give. The less we ask, the less blessings we receive.

God pours out his blessings upon us without our prayers too. As we've seen, some of his promises are unconditional. Where he assures us that he will give us the promised blessing apart from our prayers or anything else that we do.

But many promises are conditional. Like the promises of prayer. Where the promised blessing comes only to those who ask and believe. But you have to ask.

So you see, we are robbing ourselves of untold blessings when we don't ask much.

James took up this theme in his letter. In the fourth chapter he berates the recipients of his letter for their insatiable desire for pleasures. That it led to all sorts of evils. "You desire and do not have . . . You covet and cannot obtain, so you fight and quarrel."

The irony behind all this, says James, is that you could have had some of these blessing if you had just asked God: "You do not have, because you do not ask" (James 4:2).

"You don't have because you don't ask." What James wrote to these First Century believers remains true for many of us. We don't have the many blessings that God would have given us if we had just asked.

God wants you to ask so that you can have. God wants you to test his promises so that you can discover that they are true and that he always keeps them.

Why not start right now?

ABOUT THE AUTHOR

Dr. Richard P. Bucher received his Doctor of Theology degree from Boston University in 2001. He served as Pastor at Trinity Lutheran Church, Clinton, MA from 1985-2003 and at Our Redeemer Lutheran Church from 2003-2006. He served as Campus Dean and Professor at Strayer University from 2007 to 2011, and has served as an adjunct online professor since 2012. He is the author of *The Ecumenical Luther* published by Concordia Publishing House in 2003. He currently resides in Fishers, Indiana.

www.ingramcontent.com/pod-product-compliance
Lightning Source LLC
Chambersburg PA
CBHW061724020426
42331CB00006B/1086